'NICE ALTOIDS'

IBM
@too
IBM is an IBM e-business

Speed bump.
The new Turbo
Drivers wanted.

THIRD EDITION

How to Advertise

Kenneth Roman and Jane Maas
with Martin Nisenholtz

Thomas Dunne Books
St. Martin's Griffin New York

THOMAS DUNNE BOOKS.
An imprint of St. Martin's Press.

www.stmartins.com

Library of Congress Cataloging-in-Publication Data

Roman, Kenneth.
How to advertise : Third Edition / Kenneth Roman and Jane Maas with Martin Nisenholtz.—3rd ed.
p. cm.
Includes index (p. 253).
ISBN 0-312-31859-6 (hc)
ISBN 0-312-34021-4 (pbk)
EAN 978-0312-34021-6
1. Advertising. I. Maas, Jane. II. Nisenholtz, Martin. III. Title.

HF5823.R665 2003
659.1—dc21 2003053159

First Edition: 1976
Second Edition: 1992
Third Edition: September 2003
First St. Martin's Griffin Edition: March 2005

D 10 9 8

Contents

Preface

Will There Still Be Advertising?

Will there still be "advertising" in the new world of multimedia, multichannel, multi-option communications? Viewers used to "zap" ads with their remotes, now they can zoom by them with their personal video recorder.

We don't know the future of advertising—it changes too rapidly. We do know that every new technology has brought with it predictions of the demise of one medium or another. Somehow those predictions never materialized. Advertising is a creative business, and the inventiveness of people in it never ceases to amaze. Media "morph" into something more relevant, new media are invented, old media never completely go away.

The driving force behind this changing face of advertising is the underlying fact that—whatever the medium of the moment—*advertising works*. It builds brands and it sells products, and leading companies in every sector know it.

This book started with a simple proposition—to help advertisers deal with the creative product. The trick with something like this is to keep it fresh and relevant, yet not so fresh that it spoils in a few years when trends fade to fads.

It has become increasingly clear that advertising is more

than ads. Like it or not, it has become ubiquitous. It is everywhere, from the tidal wave of mailings and catalogs to the intrusion of telemarketing. Barriers between media, even between advertising and entertainment, are breaking down. TV shows include product placements, on camera or in "virtual reality." New technologies like the digital video recorder have the power to change the way we watch television—and perhaps avoid watching advertising.

The structure of the business has changed accordingly. Agencies have grown larger and agglomerated into holding companies of marketing service companies, while hot new creative boutiques seem to be born every week. Big media companies make cross-media deals with big clients. Traditional "offline" agencies have learned new media and been joined by online specialists.

Advertisers have had to adjust to integrating messages in different media into a consistent brand image. While we deal with the major media types in separate chapters, the consumer doesn't necessarily see it that way. Reading or working while watching TV or listening to radio is not a new phenomenon. There are few clean lines in the way people "consume" media (to use the lingo of the business). So we've added a chapter on integrated communications.

We were surprised (and gratified) when we updated this book in 1992, sixteen years after it was first published, by how many of our points still held true. Almost everything had changed—people, markets, creative techniques, media, technologies. But we couldn't find one *principle* of communicating with consumers that no longer seemed valid.

Had we taken on this new edition a few years ago, during the dot-com boom, we would have been told that a "new economy" was rapidly replacing "old economy" principles and practices, that New Age media companies like AOL and Yahoo! were fast eclipsing giants of the old order. We found instead that there's one economy, the one consisting of profitable businesses, and that the internet will play a fundamental role in its shape over the coming decades.

The internet has been characterized as the world's biggest library and the world's biggest marketplace. Since it is a legitimate new medium (as well as a new technology), we've added sections on internet advertising and interactive marketing, and revised other chapters to take its influence into account.

We also added a co-author with world-class credentials in new media—Martin Nisenholtz, CEO of New York Times Digital, whose contributions to this edition go well beyond the internet chapter.

More significant even than the internet are the twin revolutions of globalization and fragmentation—of markets and media. Television and the internet have made the world a smaller place and increased the role of global brands. Within this coming together, there is incredible diversity. The explosion of choice in media—hundreds of broadcast and cable channels, targeted magazine titles and radio stations—reflects the proliferation of market segments.

Advertising is about ideas. Never underestimate the power of an idea, as one campaign used to put it. Advertising must do its job legally, ethically . . . and brilliantly. So we have added a new chapter on how to encourage, recognize, and protect ideas, and strengthened the chapter on working with agencies, to underline the role of the client in producing great advertising. We also refreshed the examples of advertising we admire—enduring campaigns that build brands and businesses.

Advertising is also about results. Return on investment is more than ever an issue in business, even if no easier to measure. Advertising may be entertaining, it needs to command attention, most of all it must be accountable. These are big bucks—advertising is usually one of the largest line items in a budget. Yet too many dollars are wasted on amateur efforts that neither communicate nor sell, and often are not even measured.

Not all advertising works. Far too much money is wasted on ineffective creative work. Graham Phillips, former Chairman and CEO of Ogilvy & Mather Worldwide and Y&R Advertising, assesses the reasons as too much attention to the bottom line, fewer training programs, too much focus on winning awards that have nothing to do with generating results, insufficient involvement by senior people in the creative process, rewarding creative people for clever and cute ads instead of results for clients, and one particularly relevant factor: "clients are often not well trained on how to recognize great advertising."

This book aims to help advertisers in that task.

We start with an appreciation of David Ogilvy and his contributions to modern advertising. The most famous advertising man in the world (as he liked to remind people), David influenced our thinking at Ogilvy & Mather, and was a profound influence on the business. He was a surgeon-like editor of the original edition of this book, generously endorsed it ("worth its weight in gold") and contributed the title, and was a friend and mentor.

David taught the principle of searching for principles. From its first edition, this book has attempted to capture enduring principles of communication—principles grounded in research and marketplace success. What works, what doesn't, and why. This new edition builds on that foundation and recognizes the new challenge of building brands and businesses in a new marketing world.

Kenneth Roman
Jane Maas

Reflections on David Ogilvy

The Purpose of Advertising

From monkeys to M&M's, Madison Ave. mostly opts to entertain the Super Bowl's TV fans

—HEADLINE IN *THE NEW YORK TIMES*

Nobody was more consistently vigilant in exposing creativity for creativity's sake as a false god than David Ogilvy, the last giant of the business, who died in 1999 at the age of eighty-eight. "Who is approving this junk called advertising?" he asked DeWitt Helm, then president of the Association of National Advertisers in 1991, before firing another salvo at an ANA conference. "Have the clients gone crazy?"

Nobody was more vigorous than Ogilvy in elevating the people who create advertising. He constantly encouraged them to do brilliant work. "Unless your campaign is based on a Big Idea, it will pass like a ship in the night" was one of his frequent charges.

He accepted that advertising had to attract attention ("You can't save souls in an empty church") but not at the expense of selling a client's product. Unimpressed with the creative revolution that first emerged in the 1970s and put off by its flashy techniques with no evident payoff in sales, he delivered his message in interviews and speeches—"There is a disease called entertainment infecting our business." The disease was spread, in his view, by awards given at creative contests.

His first move, to ban Ogilvy & Mather people from entering these contests, which generally rewarded humor or dazzling production techniques, caused a minor mutiny. So he announced he was creating his own (cash) award, The David Ogilvy Award—for sales. "If you, my fellow copywriters or art directors, want to win the award, devote your genius to making the cash register ring."

His campaign did little to slow the creative contests, which in recent years have produced a noticeable increase in humor and entertainment—and bewildered viewers. "Even though the number of wacky dot-com commercials decreased [in 2000]," concluded *The Wall Street Journal* in its year-end review, "there were still plenty of odd-ball, head-scratching commercials to marvel over this year." Some of this confusion is generational, some reflects a technology gap—products or concepts that people don't understand. "Edgy" production techniques, designed to capture attention, can get in the way of the message. Whatever the cause, more advertising is just plain obscure—people can't figure out what it is saying or even what is being advertised.

Many successful people in advertising lack conventional credentials, but move through a series of eclectic experiences and find ways to draw upon these to bring fresh perspectives to the business. Ogilvy was a prime example. After being tossed out of Oxford, he went to work as a sous-chef in the Hotel Majestic in Paris. He later drew upon his experiences in the kitchen of the demanding head chef Monsieur Pitard, as his model of management—standards of hard work, discipline, and excellence.

Passing the test as a chef, but seeing little career potential in long kitchen hours, he got a job in Scotland as a salesman for Aga Cookers, stoves found in better kitchens throughout England and the Continent. Just as his views about how to lead an organization were formed in a Paris kitchen, Ogilvy's philosophy of advertising was influenced by the reception he received at the doors of Scottish housewives. Selling door-to-door made its mark. "No sale, no commission. No commission, no eat. That made an impression on me."

He was so good at selling stoves that the company assigned him to create a manual for other salesmen. Written in 1935 when Ogilvy was twenty-four years old, *The Theory and Practice of Selling the Aga Cooker* was described by *Fortune* magazine (in an article about him in 1965) as "probably the best sales manual ever written." He sent it to his elder brother Francis, managing director of the Mather & Crowther agency in London, who hired him and later sent him to the United States to study American advertising techniques.

Among his introductory letters was one to Dr. George Gallup, whose Audience Research Institute in Princeton was polling American public opinion. Ogilvy described his time with Gallup as the luckiest break of his life: "If you ever decide to seek your fortune in a foreign country, the best thing you can do is get a job with the local Gallup Poll. It will teach you what the natives want out of life, what they think are the main issues of the day. You will quickly get to know more about the country of your adoption than most of its inhabitants."

"In 1938 Mather & Crowther sent me to the United States. There I came under the influence of Claude Hopkins, a young copywriter named Rosser Reeves, John Caples and George Gallup," Ogilvy wrote in 1979, recounting the first major statement of his ideas about advertising, views that remained substantially unchanged throughout his career.

While Reeves's Unique Selling Proposition (U.S.P.) often produced abrasive advertising, Ogilvy shared Reeves's enthusiasm for advertising that sells. Caples, the preeminent mail order writer of the day, was described by Ogilvy as knowing "more about the *realities* of advertising than anyone else." George Gallup contributed to Ogilvy's education the idea of using opinion research and factor analysis to predict success.

Ogilvy especially admired Claude Hopkins, "who is to advertising what Escoffier is to cooking." In his introduction to the reissue of *Scientific Advertising*, he wrote:

> *Nobody, at any level, should be allowed to have anything to do with advertising until he has read this book seven times. Claude Hopkins wrote it in 1933. Rosser Reeves, bless him, gave it to me in 1938. Since then, I have given 379 copies to clients and colleagues. Every time I see a bad advertisement, I say to myself, "The man who wrote this copy has never read Claude Hopkins." If* you *read this book of his, you will never write another bad advertisement—and never approve one either.*

What Hopkins, Reeves, Caples, and Gallup were telling him about advertising only confirmed what he had learned selling Aga Cookers—advertising had to be judged on its ability to sell rather than entertain.

Ogilvy was ready to deliver to his associates in London findings on what he had learned. His presentation, remembered by those present as a tour de force, opened:

> *My ideas about advertising have been completely reoriented in the past year. I have experienced the*

> *biggest personal revolution of my life . . . I now know that aesthetics have nothing to do with advertising. The most important job of an ad is to centre all the attention on the merchandise and none on the technique of presenting it. Advertising has got to sell. And the worst thing about your advertising is that it lacks sales punch.*
>
> *In writing ads, act as if you met the individual buyer face to face. Don't show off. Don't try to be funny. Don't try to be clever. Don't behave eccentrically. Measure ads by salesmen's standards, not by amusement standards.*

In 1947, Francis Ogilvy proposed to S. H. Benson that they and Mather & Crowther send his brother to America to launch an agency to assist British clients in the U.S. Initially billed as research director, Ogilvy tried writing copy, was a success, and named himself Copy Chief as well. Among his early efforts were Guinness, British Travel, and Rolls-Royce, for which he wrote perhaps the most famous car headline: "At 60 miles an hour the loudest noise in this new Rolls-Royce comes from the electric clock."

Ogilvy was doing more than writing ads, he was creating brand images. "The pivotal character in discovering [branding] was David Ogilvy," writes James B. Twitchell in *Twenty Ads That Shook the World*. "Not only did he succeed in branding such parity items as tonic water (Schweppes), credit cards (American Express), dress shirts (Hathaway), soap (Dove), and gasoline (Shell), but he also pulled off the sublime coup of branding himself." These companies might object to the characterization of their products as parity. They would likely agree with Ogilvy's contention that "every advertisement should be thought of as a contribution to the brand image."

The agency's operating philosophy was taken from J. P. Morgan: "Only first-class business, and that in a first-class way." The advertising Ogilvy created followed the same principle. "It pays to give your brand a *first-class ticket* through life."

The first-class ticket Ogilvy gave his clients had a distinctive look that was easy to spot—handsome photographs (never artwork), literate headlines, and long text copy packed with facts. The advertising reeked of quality—the products advertised, the tone of the copy, and the uncluttered layouts with elegant typography.

One of his most enduring campaigns was for Lever Brothers' Dove, initially presented to the agency as the first "neutral" soap. Suspecting that consumers would have little interest in that proposition, Ogilvy discovered that one ingredient was similar to deep cleansing creams popular at that time. He proposed positioning Dove as better than soap because it contains "one-quarter cleansing cream" and doesn't dry a woman's skin. That campaign, still running forty years later, helped make Dove the leading toilet bar in the U.S.

Raymond Rubicam, the co-founder of Young & Rubicam, asked why he had never written a book, responded, "David Ogilvy took it all and put it in his book." Nothing brought more fame than the publication in 1963 of *Confessions of an Advertising Man. Confessions* became the best-selling advertising book of all time, with some 1.5 million copies published around the world. Only recently out of print after more than thirty years, it's as readable as when first published. Anything but pedantic, it distills experience into pungent principles:

You cannot bore *people into buying.*

Committees can criticize advertisements, but they cannot create them.

Compromise has no place in advertising. Whatever you do, go the whole hog.

And perhaps the most-quoted—"*The consumer is not a moron. She is your wife. Don't insult her intelligence.*" (This later changed to a more politically correct "The consumer is not a moron. Don't insult his or her intelligence.")

The Ogilvy philosophy rested on four pillars. Research. Results. Creative brilliance. Professional discipline. Ogilvy believed in studying precedents and codifying experience into principles—treating advertising as a profession with a body of knowledge.

Around this time, Bill Bernbach was leading a different revolution. His agency, Doyle Dane Bernbach, valued inspiration and witty sophisticated creative work over research. David Abbott, a respected London copywriter who cites Ogilvy as his first hero, says he found himself unable to ignore Ogilvy's rules, even after forty years. When first exposed to DDB advertising, however, "I realized there was another way of doing ads. I admired the simplicity and the impact of the art direction . . . it wasn't that different from the Ogilvy discipline, but it added something on top of that: the need to get noticed."

Don Arlett, a former O&M creative director, used to argue to Ogilvy that his sales concept was a little simplistic for modern times. "I don't think he understood the power of visual icons or the importance of art direction as communication." This may have stemmed in part from growing up in a print era and never fully understanding television.

Creative people largely gravitated to the DDB school, but many clients related to Ogilvy's approach to the business. Campbell Soup set up a David Ogilvy Award for effective advertising for their brands, confident that as judge he would be so objective the award could go to other Campbell agencies (it did). In 1994, The Advertising Research Foundation announced The David Ogilvy Research Awards "For effective use of research in developing successful advertising." In a videotape introducing the ARF awards, Ogilvy again took on the "creative entertainers":

> *Nowadays, you know, the creative departments and agencies are dominated by specialists in television. Their ambition is to win awards at festivals. They don't give a damn whether their commercials will sell, provided they entertain and win awards. They won't have anything to do with research if they can help it. These creative entertainers have done the advertising business appalling damage.*

Discouraged with the direction advertising was taking, Ogilvy turned his attention to direct marketing. He had set up a Direct Mail department in the 1960s, well before most agencies recognized its potential. Ogilvy & Mather Direct grew to be the world's largest direct marketing organization; he became its godfather. He attended its conferences with interest, calling direct mail "my first and secret love." His office in Paris was at the direct marketing agency, "my spiritual home." When O&M Direct chose as its motto, "We Sell. Or Else," it perfectly expressed his philosophy.

He never lost interest in the business and for years after an official retirement to his twelfth-century Chateau Touffou in France he continued to bombard friends and colleagues with letters and memos. He watched over careers of young agency people (especially talented young women), hosted conferences of creative directors, visited foreign offices (he particularly liked India and South Africa), met with clients, received awards for lifetime achievement, and reveled in his celebrity. He was a colorful personality with a sense for the dramatic and the outrageous, in his remarks and behavior.

Preoccupied with his legacy, he commissioned a film (decades before his death) to memorialize his achievements and philosophies, ending by saying he wanted to be remembered as a copywriter who had a few big ideas. As agency chairman, he listed himself in the telephone directory as "Copywriter."

David Ogilvy contributed a great deal more to the business than several enduring campaigns. He created the concept of brand image. He trumpeted the virtues of research, global brands, and direct marketing. He embodied values of professionalism, civilization, and good taste. The ideas he championed, now well accepted (if not always practiced), remind us of the purpose of advertising.

PART I

What to Say—and Where to Say It

1 Advertising Is About Ideas

Actor Jack Lemmon, a very average-looking guy, was said to inspire himself to rise above the ordinary by repeating a simple phrase just before he went in front of the cameras. He'd snap his fingers and say, "OK. Magic time!"

The magic of an idea is what lifts some advertising above the ordinary. No amount of dazzling production technique can cover up the absence of an underlying idea.

People try to analyze and define the creative process, with varying degrees of success. "I'm supposed to be the number one creative genius in the whole wide world," said David Ogilvy in a 1991 speech to the Association of National Advertisers, "and I don't even know what the hell the word 'creativity' means."

What we know is that ideas are precious. They are hard to come by, fragile when young, powerful when established. They change perceptions, command loyalty (and attract imitators), and build brands.

Advertising is a business of ideas. Whether or not you consider yourself creative, you must respect the creative process and understand how to work with—and inspire—creative people. It's far better if you can contribute rather than backing away with the excuse "I'm not creative."

Creative director Bill Backer makes the point that you

 don't have to be "creative" in the everyday sense of the word.

The people you think of as "creative types," like writers, artists, and advertising people, are mostly in the business of executing *ideas.*

I don't mean to imply that we are all equal when it comes to grabbing hold of good basic ideas. But we are all more equal than we think.

Sure, there are some people who just plain excel in the area of ideas. They seem to start with a God-given ability to recognize every little spark that occurs and grab hold of it. They don't necessarily write, draw, make up songs, or design clothes. They could just as easily be your electrician or the person who sold you your last car as the creative director who was your best friend growing up.

You may never be their equal, but you can develop the 'know-how' to be better than you are right now.

You can be better than you are right now.

The business of ideas—inspiring them in others and contributing—has several parts. Understanding where ideas come from. Recognizing how to protect them when they are young. Creating an environment in which they grow. Developing your own ability to personally generate ideas.

Where Ideas Come From

Benjamin Franklin, bothered by the need for two pairs of spectacles, one for distance and one for things nearby, came up with the idea for bifocals.

Successful concepts are not complicated. They are relevant and easy to understand. The best advertising ideas are frequently marketing ideas that are built into products.

The Sony Walkman added a headset to a tape player to create mobile music, for walking or jogging.

eBay combined the appeal of a flea market with the internet to create an online auction site.

These illustrate the first (and most comforting) principle—creativity doesn't create something out of nothing. It uncovers, selects, reshuffles, combines, synthesizes already existing facts, skills, and ideas. That's what Arthur Koestler, in his landmark book *The Act of Creation*, calls "bisociation," a fancy word for putting existing ideas together to create something "original"—like linking the computer to telecommunications to create the internet.

So the object is not something "new" but a new combination of existing elements. One of the founding fathers of information technology (and of Intel and miniaturization), Carver Mead claims to have never had an original idea.

Protecting New Ideas

New ideas must be protected, says management guru Peter Drucker. "The innovative company understands that innovation starts with an idea. And ideas are somewhat like babies—they are born small, immature and shapeless."

Many companies are filled with well-meaning people who can kill ideas with questions or organizational layers that filter the vitality out of an idea. The entrepreneurial company collapses management layers, tries a lot of ideas—and lets the consumer decide. It protects ideas until they mature.

Working with a creative product starts with the principle of tolerance for error. *Risk*. Outstanding creative work is original in concept and execution. Original means untried, and therefore entails risk. Risk is at the heart of creativity.

One measure of originality is its surprise effect. The more original a discovery, the more obvious it seems after the fact. When the French Impressionists first exhibited their paintings in 1874, the public found their work so disconcerting that newspaper cartoons suggested this gentle art would cause pregnant women to miscarry. Beethoven's Ninth Symphony was booed on first hearing. Matisse and his fellow artists became known as the Fauves, or "wild beasts."

Freddie Heineken's colleagues thought it a little mad when he proposed to sell Heineken beer overseas in green-glass bottles instead of the usual brown ones. The distinctive bottles helped make Heineken one of the global beer giants.

"Don't be afraid of new ideas merely because they are new," wrote Ernest St. Elmo Lewis (in 1923!) in *The Power of an Idea*, "but be afraid of old ideas because they are old—probably outworn, shoddy with use." An innovator in advertising, Hal Riney points out, "Almost every new idea brings risk."

Ideas represent change, so be prepared to be shocked if you genuinely want big ideas. Hold your fire when new work is presented. Creative people are intuitive and often "get there before the rest of us," explains an agency executive.

Don't start by evaluating the idea or expecting it to be perfect. All you want is a germ of something that can grow. Separate the evaluation of ideas from their generation. There's always time to ask questions later.

Look for lots of ideas. The odds of hitting the single big one are low, so it pays to generate many, possibly unconventional, ideas to refine and measure.

Create an Environment for Ideas

Ideas can appear anywhere—Harvey Fierstein wrote his *Torch Song Trilogy* on the subway to Brooklyn. Big offices with mahogany panels seem almost anti-creative. Walk into the creative department of many advertising agencies, and you'll find Ping-Pong tables, walls to write on, colorful graphics, and, especially, informal gathering areas where writers congregate with art directors and producers. There have long been such areas at Hallmark, which boasts the world's largest creative department.

"Being a creative is a pretty insecure business," says Peter Warren, former head of Ogilvy & Mather in Europe. "The fear of drying up and not meeting deadlines is ever present, so the more one can protect individuals, groups, and departments from those pressures, the better in terms of their productive output. In my experience, the departments that are the most productive invariably have plenty of laughter in the halls and a strong *esprit de corps.*"

The problem is usually not ideas, but making them happen.

Don Arlett, a top London creative director, used his interest in gardening to explain how to create the right environment. You can buy the best plants and plant them in the garden, he said, but they won't do well unless you prepare the soil properly, provide water, sun, and space, and feed them from time to time.

> *A consistently high standard of creative work can only exist in an atmosphere that makes it possible. That happens when all the people in the agency genuinely want to work toward high creative goals and are prepared to bear the responsibility for making them happen.*

Some agencies are good at marketing, but seem unable to produce outstanding creative work. They may hire talented writers and art directors, but the work never sparkles. They haven't grasped that great advertising is not just the job of the creative department.

So what's the role of the client in all this?

First, create the right environment by showing everyone that you care about great creative work. Spend time with the agency creative people, not just the account managers. Recognize them when they deliver. Make it clear to your organization that you are prepared to encourage and defend ideas—and that you will judge them in part on the quality of the creative work.

Advertising is a collaborative process—between copywriter and art director or producer, between client and agency. It's rare that an agency goes off alone and creates a great campaign.

"The uncreative mind can spot the wrong answers," wrote Anthony Jay in *Management and Machiavelli*. "It takes a creative mind to spot the wrong questions." The right question can make all the difference. Great campaigns almost invariably emerge when a client asks a big question and challenges the agency to come up with a big solution.

Know what you want. The worst clients are those who give no direction, but just hope the agency will strike lightning. Asking for something that is "cool" or "edgy" is not enough. What do you mean by "breakthrough"?

What you mean by "great"? Something that gets talked about—or a campaign that builds a brand? What about abrasive advertising that sells—or award-winning ads that people remember and like but don't act upon? Nirvana is ideas that consumers notice and find compelling.

Generating Ideas

There are books on producing ideas but no sure-fire technique that works for everyone. David Ogilvy favored immersing himself in background reading, then in a bottle of wine to let his subconscious go to work. A Boston newspaperman used to write a popular column called "Thoughts While Shaving." Ideas often emerge in the bathroom—in the shower, while shaving, doing something routine and letting the mind drift.

Archimedes was said to have found the principle of buoyancy in a bath, and Newton found gravity while musing under an apple tree. The man who invented Velcro came up with the idea while walking through a field and noticing the burrs that stuck to his legs. Ideas don't always come out of the blue. It helps to be on the lookout for them. As Pasteur observed, "Chance favors the prepared mind."

Journalist Alan Hall, musing over a long liquid lunch, came up with the idea of the annual race to ship newly bottled Beaujolais Nouveau to Britain, "the greatest marketing stroke since the end of World War II" said *Figaro,* the French daily. Virginia Woolf said she often received her inspirations for writing while in the bath.

The conscious use of the subconscious is more than hoping for inspiration. It is a process, writes James Webb Young (*A Technique for Producing Ideas*) that requires practice.

It starts with gathering raw material—reading and listening. One of the best things you can do is to get out of the office and into the field. Talk with customers and observe them. Write down ideas (even crazy or incomplete). Keep a notepad by your bedside. *Then sleep on it.* Let the subconscious go to work, and ideas will usually emerge.

The ability to see relationships is an important part of the process. Try to identify similarities that can lead to new ideas.

The first principle of toy marketing—make the product fun—applied to the hamburger business helped create the Fun Meal for McDonald's.

Analogies are a useful way to generate ideas, even with dissimilar businesses.

Observing similarities between the structure of the beer and coffee businesses, Maxwell House translated the success of imported beers to create Maxwell House French Roast.

Consider "brainstorming"—free-associating in a group with a moderator to capture the ideas and enforce the rules. No judging (all ideas are good at this stage). Judging comes later.

There is a view that traditional brainstorming produces irrelevant or hard-to-implement ideas. Jacob Goldenberg, a professor at Hebrew University in Jerusalem, feels that people sometimes need a road map as they seek new ways of thinking and new frameworks for shaping ideas. Taking a method developed for solving engineering problems and applying it to product development and advertising campaigns, he has identified five "creative templates."

- *Changing a key variable*—wet diapers that generate a strong but pleasant scent to let parents know baby needs a change, for example.
- *Looking at how a product is linked to its environment*—Post-it notes answers the question "How can writers link their notes to where they want them to be seen?"
- *Substituting part of a product*—using a car's radio speaker to replace a dedicated cell phone speaker (saving space and improving sound quality).
- *Displacing a component*—removing the recording function from the Walkman to squeeze in more high-quality playback.
- *Splitting one product into two*—separating shampoo from conditioner.

How you ask the question counts. Are you looking at the market too narrowly?

Oreo cookies opened opportunities beyond the cookie market by defining Oreo taste, which could be applied to ice cream, cereals, milkshakes, pie crust.

"In innovation as in any other endeavor there is talent, there is ingenuity, and there is knowledge," notes Peter Drucker. "But when all is said and done, what innovation requires is hard, focused, purposeful work."

Perhaps the hardest part of the work is still to come. No matter how brilliant, ideas don't sell themselves. They have to be *sold*—relentlessly, continually, and creatively. An idea is not an idea until it is sold.

The Accenture consulting group recognizes this in a campaign that promises "Innovation Delivered."

The illustration—a wave rolling onto a beach. The headline—"I am your idea. One day you'll look for me and I'll be gone."

The sub-headline: "It's not how many ideas you have, it's how many you make happen."

The Magic of Ideas

Two journalists talked about working on a biography of Theodor Geisel, creator of the Dr. Seuss books. They pushed him to explain the creative process.

"Drawing was easy, he said, for him; the sweat came from writing. He said, 'I stay with a line until the meter is right and the rhyme is right, even if it takes five hours. Sometimes I go counter to the clock.'

"Ted at that point went silent and looked as if he were dazed. Finally, he said, 'I don't understand what I just said, do you?' We said, 'No.' He said, 'Well, that's it; that's the creative process.' The subject was closed."

Magic is, well, magic. Not always rational.

2 Brands and Strategies

Strategy has to inform everything you do. Everything that a company does—from the way it paints its trucks, to how long it takes to answer your telephones, to what people in your factories tell their friends—communicates with the public.

Strategies beget brands, and brands in today's marketplace transcend products. Brands are much more than what you eat or drink or brush your teeth with. Brand strategy is the summation of all your communications.

—SERGIO ZYMAN, *THE END OF MARKETING AS WE KNOW IT*

The power of a strong brand is vivid in the photo of a muscled arm tattooed with the Harley-Davidson logo. The headline: "When was the last time you felt as strongly about anything as this?"

Brands began as guarantors of reliability and quality in consumer products, and have evolved into representations of a way of life or a set of ideas—as Nike's "swoosh" logo and advertising evoke personal achievement.

 Companies too can become brands in having a personality and set of values. Think of IBM or Apple, computer makers with very different identities. Yet customers of each company are loyal to their brand and trust its products.

Some talk about this as "brand essence," "brand DNA," or "brand promise" (the promise you are making to the consumer).

Boeing formalized its first-ever brand strategy to reach beyond the commercial airline business. Everything from its logo to the decision to relocate its headquarters from Seattle to Chicago has been done with the Boeing brand in mind. Even meat packers like Hormel and Swift are developing brands in what used to be an unbranded category, just as Purdue did with chickens.

Brands encourage consumer loyalty and command premium pricing. They compress data, communicate quickly, and simplify buying decisions.

A brand is more than a name and a means of identification. It is a set of added values that offer functional and psychological benefits to the consumer, values signaled in consumer products by packaging, price, color, taste, smell, or shape.

When asked what was most important to Starbucks' success—the coffee, the stores, the people working behind the counters—chief coffee guru Dave Olsen replied, "Everything matters."

And advertising! Building brand equity—and selling products—is what advertising is about. A product's advertising is very much a part of its identity.

Strategies

Strategies are the foundation on which brands are built. They keep the advertising and other marketing elements on track and build a clear and consistent personality.

 They represent the soul of a brand and a crucial element in success.

If your strategy is right, if the promise and core benefit is going to strike the consumer in the head or heart or gut, and if your advertising clearly communicates that promise—you're a long way toward home.

The first thing to look for in advertising is the key consumer benefit or the core idea—the heart of the strategy. It must leap out at you from the page or the storyboard or radio script and grab you by the jugular. Before you look at new advertising, review the strategy—*every time.*

A creative brief relates the strategy to the current situation and objectives. At its worst, a creative brief baffles the creative team with vague statements and catch phrases. At its best, it guides with a tightly defined strategy and stimulates with a large goal. The team should say, "I get it."

WHAT GOES INTO A STRATEGY?

Strategy documents differ in form and terminology, but most cover these major points:

What Is Our Objective?

What action do we want consumers to take? The most frequent answer is "We want them to buy the product."

> *Ads urged consumers to try the Dove beauty bar regimen for 14 days and compare the results to the soap they were using.*

Strategy statements sometimes have other objectives, such as "Take the car on a test drive" or "Use the can of soup sitting on the kitchen shelf" or "Energize the sales force."

Who Are We Talking to?

If you try to talk to everyone, you're not talking directly to anyone. The broader your target, the blander your message. You need a portrait of the target audience's attitudes and usage patterns—beyond mere demographics.

Dove targets women twenty-five years and older who believe they have dry skin. This section of the strategy marries demographics (age) with psychographics (perceptions and attitudes).

What Is the Key Consumer Benefit or Core Idea?

The one single idea we want the target audience to take out of the advertising.

Dove does not dry your skin the way other soaps can.

What Is the Reason for the Consumer to Believe What We Say?

What makes us different from others who make the same claim?

Dove is one-quarter moisturizing lotion.

What Should Be Our Tone and Manner?

What is the personality of the brand? Does it need reinforcement or change?

Dove's personality is always real, always honest.

Evolving a Strategy

Advertising is the art of delivering a sales proposition in an attention-getting, involving vehicle and positioning the product uniquely in the consumer's mind.

A creative brief presents the situation *now*—competition, market conditions, media considerations, etc. The brief brings the strategy to life and gives the creative team important insights. Some strategy elements change over time as markets and consumers change. The positioning—and the strategy—is for "all time."

Dove beauty bar's reason-why was evolved over the years. As deep cleansing cream came to be seen as old-fashioned, it changed from "one-quarter cleansing cream" to "one-quarter moisturizing lotion." The promise of softer, younger skin never changed.

Two Secret Ingredients—Quality and Emotion

Advertising works best if it is selling a product that is better than competition. It is not a cosmetic to cover up deficiencies in quality. "Advertising a bad product," said ad man Bill Bernbach, "only makes it fail faster."

The success of Procter & Gamble is often misattributed to big budgets that overwhelm other advertisers. The secret of P&G's winning brands lies more in a fundamental commitment to develop and maintain superior products. P&G will not introduce a new product unless the company is convinced it is better than competition. Once in the market, the product is continually improved to keep it preferred versus competition. P&G management states it does not believe in product life cycles and claims to have made fifty-five significant modifications in Tide in the thirty years following this brand's introduction. This confidence in their product superiority leads to the confidence to invest in large advertising and sampling programs.

> *The key to successful marketing is superior product performance. If the consumer does not perceive any real benefits in the brand, then no amount of ingenious advertising and selling can save the brand.*
>
> —ED HARNESS, FORMER P&G CHAIRMAN

P&G is also notable in its dedication to build emotion into its rational promises.

- *Dawn dishwashing liquid promised grease-free dishes so clean they reflected—"A nice reflection on you."*
- *Sure deodorant was introduced with the rational promise of dry underarms, couched in advertising that showed people raising their arms—with confidence.*

Appeal to the heart as well as the mind.

WHY BRANDS FAIL

Brands fail for many reasons—bad products, bad research, bad pricing, bad luck, and bad advertising. But the reason most brands fail is bad thinking, which really means bad strategies. It pays to be skeptical about strategy statements, to look at them critically rather than approvingly. The fact that you have conscientiously filled out a strategy statement does not make it right.

Here are some pitfalls to watch for.

Don't Lose Sight of Your Consumer

A British cable executive, asked why interactive TV had so much more success in the UK and European Union than in the U.S., replied, "You always try to build a better mousetrap. We ask the mouse what he likes to eat."

How does your product fit with the consumer's attitudes, needs, and lifestyle? Most strategies focus too much on the product, too little on the consumer. Instead of parading product attributes, talk about consumer benefits.

Don't Rely on Research Alone

Research is an aid to judgment, not the whole answer. Do the conclusions make sense based on what you know and observe?

Even numbers can be misleading.

A Huggies diaper commercial showed a man holding a baby, then making a face and groaning "Uh-oh!" It broke records in recall testing but didn't move the brand.

A new strategy—a dry baby is a happy baby—made the baby the center of the attention and helped build Huggies into the leading diaper brand. Commercials now show diaper-clad babies doing adult things. One shows a baby with umbrella, with background music: "I'm singing in the rain. What a glorious feeling. I'm happy again."

Dig into the research. Check the sample size—is it large enough to be representative? How were the issues framed to the consumer?

Don't Give Up the High Ground

In most categories there is one benefit more meaningful than any other—the high ground. It's what people ultimately buy the product for and what must be salient in the advertising. In laundry detergents, it's clean. In cold medicines, relief.

People buy diet soft drinks in part to reduce sugar intake and control weight. But the reason for buying a particular brand is taste, the high ground. "Diet Coke—just for the taste of it."

Procter & Gamble is a master at positioning its brands on the high ground. It introduced White Cloud, a toilet tissue, as "the softest tissue in the world" at the same time its own Charmin had the leading position built on the promise "squeezably soft." Any competitor wanting to enter that category would be faced with two brands on the high ground position.

Don't Belabor the Obvious

Convenience, for example, is quickly communicated and easily understood.

What is obvious about "Instant" products is that they are convenient. What is important is how they taste or perform. That should be the focus of the advertising.

Don't Use Price as a Strategy

Like convenience, low price is easy to understand. More important, few products have become long-term successes on the basis of price. There's always someone who will sell cheaper. Sooner or later, people buy quality.

Products must provide consumer value—a combination of price and quality. A cheap car that falls apart in a few years and is hard to resell is a poor value. A luxury automobile that doesn't require much maintenance and commands a good resale price is a good value. Value is a combination of quality and price.

Don't Use Popularity as a Strategy

There's not much consumer benefit in telling people that you sell a lot of your product (although it does make the advertiser feel good).

> *If coffee was the largest selling grocery product and Maxwell House the largest brand, why not tell people that and suggest they get on the bandwagon? Both client and agency loved a commercial called "America's National Drink." It failed with consumers.*

Popularity of a brand is a result, not a reason-why. It's hard to find examples of enduring success based on a leadership strategy.

Don't Forget to Offer a Benefit

Thousands of people buy quarter-inch drill bits, not because they want quarter-inch drill bits but because they want quarter-inch holes. People don't buy products—they buy expectation of benefits. Don't confuse product attributes with benefits.

Speed in a copier is an attribute. The benefit is saving time.

Heavy-duty brass couplings in a garden hose is an attribute. Seals tight is the benefit.

Don't Walk Away from a Winner

People have ingrained attitudes about your brand. Don't let "improvements" change them. Line extensions and product improvements should always make a brand *more* of what you say it is, never something less or different.

Dove beauty bar was successfully introduced as better for your skin than soap. Dove dishwashing liquid, launched years later, failed. The advertising promised it would "soften hands while you do dishes," but the harsh detergent image muddied the brand.

The Dove name was successfully used to introduce several varieties of bar soap, body washes, facial cleansing cloths, even deodorants (with moisturizers). They work because they are consistent with the brand image.

Don't change strategy lightly, even when shifts in attitude or slipping sales tell you something is wrong. The problem could be the product or competition or market conditions. Changing strategy for the wrong reasons only makes the problem worse; then you won't know what to fix.

A long-term winning strategy should be the *last* thing to change, not the first.

Saying things in a strategy doesn't make it so. Is there anything in the strategy that will alter how customers and prospects see the brand?

- Do we want users to use it more or do we want to attract nonusers (or both)?
- Whose behavior do we want to change?
- What message will make them change attitudes and behavior?
- Are we dealing with tangible product benefits, emotional benefits, or just feelings?

There must be *something* in a strategy—it can be in anything from the promise to the tone and manner—that gives evidence for believing.

Convincing young children not to experiment with drugs started with the discovery that authority figures—athletes, for example—weren't convincing. Kids consider themselves smart and able to handle the drug. Showing kids that the dealers considered them easy marks and were laughing at them proved to be a more effective strategy.

Merely saying something is good or bad is affirmation, not proof. That's what must be built into the strategy.

TEN STRATEGY CHECKPOINTS

1. Be single-minded. The essence of positioning is sacrifice. You have to give up some points to make the important ones stand out.

While New York has plenty of tourist attractions, the "I Love New York" campaign successfully promoted tourism with its single-minded focus on Broadway theater, which research showed had the greatest appeal to visitors.

All the great success stories are simple, not complicated. They say one thing—brilliantly.

Strategy is triage. You have to throw some people overboard to save others in an overcrowded lifeboat. Differentiation is standing for something, not for everything.

2. Make it fit an overall plan. Don't let product, price, or package go off in one direction while the advertising goes in another.

> *Everything about Apple's Macintosh computer was designed to be simple and user-friendly, from the product to the owner's manual and the advertising—"A computer for the rest of us."*

Watch out for dissonance between the product and the message.

3. Keep your objectives reasonable. Overambition is the pitfall of most strategies. Don't ask people to change deeply ingrained habits. Behavior can be changed—consumers go to self-service gas stations and many have learned to bank online, but it's generally easier to get people to change brands.

There's an apocryphal story about an ad touting a product that can be used as a cake ingredient or a floor polish. Don't try to be all things to all people or to sell a product for all occasions. Objectives must be reasonable.

4. Make your strategy easy to use. It should be very short, very sharp, and leave no room for misunderstanding. One page—with as much backup rationale as you need. If you can't get a creative brief on one page, the chances for a clear thirty-second commercial are slim. It's not called "brief" for nothing.

5. Decide where your business will come from. Unless you have a product that brings new users into the market, your business will have to come from an existing brand or category.

NutraSweet and Equal were positioned as replacements for sugar rather than replacing artificial sweeteners like Sweet'n Low, a much smaller market.

Pick the larger, easier target.

6. Make a meaningful promise to the consumer. The promise is a summary statement of the benefits of a product. It can be objective or subjective, rational, or emotional, or a combination of these.

"You're in the Pepsi Generation" captured a younger audience by promising a desirable self-image as well as taste and refreshment. Britney Spears added freshness to Pepsi's promise of "For those who think young."

Search for emotional benefits as well as rational points of difference.

Q-tips' rational promise was safety—50 percent more cotton at the very tip. The emotional benefit—mothers wanted the very best for their babies.

Slogans have been described as the art of advertising on the head of a pin.

"FedEx—The world on time."

"Bell Helmets—Courage for your head."

7. Understand the importance (or unimportance) of your product. There are "badge" products that say something about you as an individual. The car you drive, the beer you drink. "Low interest" categories (such as the brand of rice you serve) say little about you as an individual.

Don't kid yourself—most consumers generally are not thinking about your brand.

8. Set yourself apart. Billions of dollars have been spent behind each of these six words—*new, white, cool, power, refreshing, relief.* Why should the consumer believe you?

After studying introductions of hundreds of new products, the A. C. Nielsen Company concluded that the second brand entering a market typically gains only half the share of the pioneer brand. To succeed, the second brand must be *significantly* better or spend *significantly* more in advertising.

Make your promise convincing.

9. Relate the unknown to the known. With a new product, you must give people a frame of reference (unless it is obvious).

> *Country Time powdered drink mix was introduced as a convenient way to get "the taste of good old-fashioned lemonade."*

Tell people what your product replaces, and why it is better.

10. Keep your strategy up to date. Consumers and markets change. Don't damage the essence of what your brand stands for, but don't stand still if things are changing.

> *When Quaker Oats was repositioned from a stodgy, old-fashioned cereal into a contemporary breakfast, the brief could have said, "Take the brand out of bedroom slippers and into Nikes."*

Corporate Advertising

In many ways, corporate advertising is harder to do well than product advertising. It deals with concepts and ideas, and tends to be unspecific and obscure. Somebody said that corporate advertising should answer three questions:

- What are they saying?
- Why are they saying it to me?
- What do they want me to do about it?

Much corporate advertising doesn't get by the first question.

The best corporate advertising is usually strong product advertising—the image of American Express was largely built by advertising the American Express Card, not a "corporate" campaign. In any case, people generally don't "buy" companies.

Brand Loyalty

Brand loyalty has been declining. There are more competitors, more consumer choices, less product differentiation, more places to buy, and more media channels.

What has emerged in this ocean of messages is megabrands, strong brands with related line extensions to extend their reach. Market research firm Gartner Inc. calls this "brand-morphing," companies relying on brand strength to enter new markets.

The Virgin brand was initially linked to entertainment—specifically music, until the mid-1980s, when Virgin Atlantic was formed. That was just the beginning of its brand explosion.

Virgin aligns its brand so consumers associate Virgin with fun, entertaining and always an "experience." Virgin Atlantic launched in 1984 with a group of pop stars and journalists as passengers for its first flight from the UK to the U.S.

The Virgin Atlantic brand was expanded to Virgin Holidays, using a similar approach emphasizing fun, entertainment and the "Virgin experience." There are now over 200 media, travel, and entertainment businesses in the Virgin Group.

The resilience of strong brands enables them to hang on even when companies lose their way, as IBM and Apple did at one point. It takes a long time to build a consumer brand—and a long time to kill one.

Making It Happen

Strategy is half the game, execution—making it happen—is the other half.

That's the rest of this book.

3 Research

How do you know if your advertising is working—or that it is even saying the right thing to the right people in the first place? That's the role of research, and there are new tools to help get the answers.

The internet has revolutionized quantitative research. When lots of respondents are needed, as in advertising tracking studies, research via the web is rapidly replacing telephone surveys.

There are several reasons for the change. First of all, voice mail, Caller ID, and a climbing refusal rate have made it more difficult and more expensive than ever to do telephone research. The internet lets you reach bigger samples, faster. The Harris Interactive research firm has seven million people in its database, Decision Analyst has four million; other research companies weigh in with a million or more. If necessary, you can complete a study in just one day. There's no way you can draw on such big numbers with telephone or any other polling method.

The internet offers creative capabilities the telephone did not—you can show respondents a print ad, an out-of-home poster, or a logo, and take it away again. You can more easily get an adequate sample of hard-to-find individuals, such as women in their third trimester of pregnancy.

There was one big question everyone asked early on—

 is the internet representative of the population? It wasn't at first, but is now becoming so. Further, many research firms were careful to conduct parallel research for a year or more, running internet and telephone surveys side-by-side to prove the results were the same.

No matter what method you use to gain information, there are still basically three kinds of advertising research.

- *Strategic research*—to help identify strategic selling ideas and define the target audience before creative work begins.
- *Ad testing*—to examine individual advertisements for their ability to deliver the message.
- *In-market research*—to track the effect of a campaign over time.

Qualitative and quantitative research also play different roles.

Qualitative research can help clarify the positioning for a product, generate hypotheses, identify strategic selling ideas, and define the target audience. It can also give you a rough idea as to whether an advertisement is communicating the message. The most popular forms of qualitative research continue to be focus groups and one-on-one in-depth interviews. But verify qualitative explorations, especially positioning, with quantitative studies.

Quantitative research confirms hypotheses with the weight of numbers. You can use quantitative research to decide whether to produce a particular ad or campaign, as well as to track the effects of your campaign in the marketplace.

STRATEGIC RESEARCH

It pays to invest the most time and money up front, before the creative process begins—not after all the time and money has been spent. And the place to start is not, as happens too often, with the message, but with the potential consumers.

- Who are your best prospects?
- What do they think about your product (and your competitors')?
- What needs and wants can your product fill; how does it fit into your prospective consumers' lives?

Defining the Target Audience

Once you decide on your best prospects, and why your product appeals to them, it is easier to decide what to say.

Consumer segments, even for mass market products, are increasingly fragmenting into niches, each with its own characteristics. Most advertisers today have considerable information available in-house to begin to isolate attractive market segments.

An automobile maker may know that safety is an important feature to a broad spectrum of consumers. However, it might identify subgroups from "Timid Tillies" and "Family Outings" to "Avid Adventurers" in order to find out which are its best prospects.

You can also buy syndicated data services, such as Simmons or MRI, that provide demographic, product usage, and some life-style information. A geo-demographic system like PRIZM, a service of Claritas, describes sixty-two different lifestyle types or clusters, which can be located by zip code. These are categorized by colorful category names—Urban Gold Coast, Country Squires, Blue Blood Estates, Shotguns & Pickups.

Retailers and restaurants find site location and mapping tools particularly helpful in discovering where their consumers cluster. The owner of one fast-food franchise says: "They not only told me what part of town to open my store, they said the southeast corner would generate more traffic than the southwest. And it did!"

Another syndicated segmentation—by attitude—is available through VALS (Values and Life-Styles), originally developed by the Stanford Research Institute. VALS is a means of defining segments of consumers and linking their behavior to their values. The VALS segmentation sorts consumers into eight different lifestyle types, each according to psychological attitudes, financial resources, and general outlook on life. It can help advertisers target their best potential customers.

When research money is limited, a common approach is to use syndicated sources to get a general feel for the market and to supplement this knowledge with smaller, nonquantitative research on specific questions.

Identifying the Selling Message

You are ready for the next step—deciding what to say.

Focus groups can help to identify positioning options, suggest selling messages, and even supply specific language that can be used in advertising. A skilled moderator leads a handful of people chosen from your target audience, focusing on issues you select. Perceptive creative people love to attend focus groups because they know great campaign ideas are often born there.

In focus groups for Oreo, participants were invited to enjoy the cookies. The creative team watched people rotate the outside layers to get at the icing inside, while talking about the special ritual involved in "unlocking" and eating Oreos. These insights led to a successful campaign: "Unlock the Magic."

If you have the time and the budget, *always* do qualitative work in person, not over the internet. Most people talk better than they write. Watching body language often provides insights. And for creative people, a round of focus groups can be a powerful stimulus.

However, qualitative internet research is also growing, especially for sensitive products, topics, and services where relative anonymity is important. "Time-extended Online Focus Groups," a new development, extends the sessions over a five-to-ten-day period. The extra time helps to make up for the lack of face-to-face detail.

You'll want your agency creative team to attend the groups. If they can't be there in person, you can often arrange for videoconferencing. Networks of focus group facilities have sprung up across the country, replacing many of the smaller mom-and-pops. Most have the ability to videotape the group and beam it simultaneously to you and the agency, wherever you are. This way, you are all still part of the process, and able to communicate with the moderator.

Focus group recruiting is more sophisticated then ever. You seldom find groups that represent simply men or women of varying ages and incomes. Psychographics play an important role—you will probably want to recruit respondents who belong to attitudinal groups you have already identified.

Another new wrinkle in qualitative research is anthropological or ethnographic research. The researcher spends days and days living at home with the family, observing how they eat and sleep, cook their meals, brush their teeth.

Group moderator Mindy Goldberg almost always gives respondents "homework" to prepare before they come to the session. She often sends them paper, paste, and scissors, and asks them to create a collage, using scrap art from magazines or stick drawings to describe how they feel about a certain product or service category. She might give them a disposable camera to take photos of how a product or service is used in their home.

This exercise helps respondents "focus" on the topic and clarify their own feelings before the group begins.

Take care! These groups are not representative of a broader population sample. They can be swayed by a strong participant or a strong moderator, and can be misleading. Focus groups can often be a disaster check, but they cannot reliably predict success. Ideas from group sessions must be validated by quantitative research.

Quantitative research is statistically projectible. Qualitative research is not. "Promise testing" or "benefit testing," one reliable and fairly inexpensive form of quantitative research to guide strategy development, takes a number of possible benefits and asks consumers from the target audience two sets of questions:

- Is this benefit or "promise" important?
- Can the brand uniquely fulfill the promise?

Your brand may have a unique benefit, but one that is not important—like better handles on a lawn mower. Include disguised promises from your competitor's advertising, and don't forget emotional promises as well as rational ones.

Promises are usually presented in simple statements without illustration. Concept testing takes the strategy development process a step further with illustrations and a description of the product or service. How will it fit into a person's life? Who will use it? How should it be positioned?

AD TESTING

The purpose of ad testing should be principally how well the advertisement communicates the strategy. You may want to use a range of measures to evaluate an advertisement, in rough or finished form, and learn how to improve it. Any good researcher will tell you that the measures you use should relate to the specific *objectives* of your advertising.

Resist the slavish use of one system every time.

> *"Research today is a lot less rigid than it used to be. There is less compartmentalizing into separate tests for communication or recall, and more emphasis on how the consumer responds (or doesn't respond) to advertising and other sources of information. Most advertising has components of awareness, persuasion, branding, information and likeability that work in different ways over time."*
>
> —JERRY THOMAS, CEO OF DECISION ANALYST INC.

The best use of research money is to test your advertising in rough form, before you have spent a lot of money in production. You can use the internet to test creative work in its earliest stages. These can be simply the description of a concept, a tagline, or rough creative work such as print ads, out-of-home posters, radio scripts, and television storyboards. Since most new computers will have a media player, internet testing will offer the ability to test commercials in finished form.

Among the measures you can test for:

Communication of main ideas. Does the target audience get the message? Is the advertising saying what you want it to say, simply and directly? Is there anything missing? Likes? Dislikes? Respondents can even suggest possible improvements.

Attention value. Does the ad or commercial grab viewers or readers and make them want to watch longer or read on?

Persuasion or purchase intent. Does the advertisement impact whether or not respondents will buy the brand? Does it cause a shift in attitude to make them feel more positive about it? Or possibly more negative?

The leaders in copy testing—The ARS Group, McCollum Spielman, Decision Analyst, IPSOS-ASI, and Mapes & Ross—all have validated studies that show the relationship between their persuasion measures and sales results. In addition, they have identified factors, such as a strong consumer benefit clearly delivered, that tend to mean higher scores.

> *SmithKline Beecham Consumer Healthcare relies on ARS persuasion testing, using a measure that has been validated with in-market performance in over 2,000 cases. Recent research has shown that 94 percent of ads have* some *positive effect on sales, although the size of the impact varies hugely depending on persuasion scores.*

IN-MARKET RESEARCH

The true test is how consumers respond to the advertising in the market, with all the pressures of real-life competition, clutter, and other marketing variables such as consumer promotions and publicity.

Tracking studies continuously monitor your brand and your advertising, your competitors' brands and their advertising, for awareness, brand image, attitudes, past brand purchases, purchase intentions, and message recall. This kind of study can evaluate a new campaign or tell you whether an existing campaign is building your sales as well as building your brand—or whether your competition is doing something better. Normally, an advertising tracking study occurs in "waves" every three to six months over a period of years.

Don't walk away from a successful long-running campaign just because you think it's time for a change, or because you are bored with it. Consumers may just be starting to respond to it.

GOOD RESEARCH IMPROVES THE ODDS

Here are ten principles that can improve your chance of getting reliable information:

1. **Define success in advance.** Establish action standards up front, against which success can be evaluated. Give the researcher a clear description of the problem to be solved, not the way you think the research should be done. What are you trying to find out?

2. **Get the right sample.** Conduct testing among prime prospects for your product, but don't neglect current users. Include them in the target audience so you know how they might be different.

3. **Use the appropriate interview technique.** Focus groups can generate ideas for quantitative validation.

One-on-one in-depth interviews, while more expensive, eliminate any group bias, and can yield in-depth understanding.

Mail surveys, while inexpensive, must be validated with personal interviews to make sure the mail results are not misleading. People who fill out questionnaires may be different from people who don't.

Internet research gives you the flexibility of testing concepts or rough creative work among a small group, conducting quantitative studies with hundreds of your prime prospects, or tracking your advertising in the marketplace.

4. Test in the right environment. Whatever you are testing, choose an appropriate environment. That might be television programming, the web, in-store, even in-flight on an airplane. If you are testing two different advertisements, use the same media.

5. Test the most representative message. Don't test a double-page spread if a single-page unit is the primary one in your media plan. (Spreads seldom test twice as well as pages, but may have other values.) Similarly, if you plan to run chiefly 15-second commercials, this is the length you should test, not 30-second ones.

6. Test alternatives. You may be surprised to find the sure winner loses to another approach. Force yourself—and the agency—to look at more than one solution.

7. Make sure the advertising is the only thing that changes. This is not the time to try a new package, a new price, or a new spending level. Control all variables other than the advertising or you'll never know what the advertisement contributed.

8. Remember that people buy products, not advertising. Make sure they react as consumers, not as experts on advertising. Be careful about asking people their opinion about your *advertising*—get their reaction to your *brand*.

There are many ways to conduct the research so consumers are not aware that they are taking part in a test. Researchers may send a 30-minute video to a panel of respondents, who are asked to evaluate the pilot for a new television program. Later, they are questioned about the commercials they saw on the tape. In the same way, consumers may be invited to look over the "dummy" of a new magazine idea, but are later asked about advertisements placed in it.

One method for testing rough radio spots may be the

most ingenious of all. Consumers come to take part in a focus group. They are seated in the waiting room, with no magazines to read and nothing to do but listen to a radio program, complete with commercials.

The best option is testing on-air or in magazines while respondents are at home, doing what they normally do.

9. Be careful with numbers. Remember that the score is an approximation, and its reliability depends on the size of the sample. With a typical sample size of 150, a recall score of 22 is not necessarily higher than a 20—it's the same thing statistically. Ask the researchers how large a numerical difference indicates a real difference in the score.

10. Go beyond the numbers. Pay attention not just to scores but also to rich diagnostic information like verbatim comments. These can give you clues as to how people react and why. What does the research say about the strengths and weaknesses of the idea you are testing?

There is no magic formula for truly superior advertising. If you slavishly use learning from advertising tests as a prescription for creative work, it may lead to above-average testing scores—and mediocre advertising.

There's No Substitute For Judgment

In the final analysis, you can't rely totally on the numbers. They must be interpreted and understood in their full dimension, along with other information. Sometimes it pays to go with a lower score on one dimension (e.g., recall) if the advertisement has other long-term brand values.

Use common sense. Sometimes the data just doesn't square with reality, or people may not be willing to tell the truth.

Research is one part of the answer. Judgment is the other part.

4 Campaigns

Stars win games, teams win championships. Strong ads sell products, campaigns build brands. Think of any successful brand. You can almost always call to mind the campaign that built it:

- *"Just do it"—Nike*
- *"No cavities"—Crest*
- *"Think different"—Apple*

Each of these campaigns helped build a brand recognized around the world.

They did it with many different individual advertising executions in a variety of media. What they have in common is consistent and coordinated programs in all media over a long period of time. Brilliant one-shots make an impact and may work in the short-term. Building a brand is a team effort over many seasons.

THREE ELEMENTS THAT MAKE A CAMPAIGN

The essential ingredient of a campaign is a consistent look or feel. You should almost be able to look at a campaign and guess what is coming next. A campaignable idea points the way to fresh but related future advertisements.

Visual Similarity

The Energizer Bunny symbolizes the battery that lasts and lasts.

UPS capitalizes on the familiar brown uniform of its drivers with a brown color background in its ads (underscored by the line, "What Can BROWN Do For You?")

Insurance companies discovered the metaphor as a campaign visual—Allstate's "good hands" (for personal service), Prudential's Rock of Gibraltar (for strength and stability), Nationwide's blanket (for "blanket coverage").

A distinctive-looking product like Hershey's Kisses can be a unifying element. The Kiss is the sole campaign visual—with variations on this theme.

Print

- *A single foiled-wrapped Kiss—"Get out the good silver."*
- *Four autumn-colored Kisses—"Fall foliage."*
- *Two intertwined Kisses—"Be mine—Happy Valentine's Day from Hershey's."*

Television

- *Two Kisses dancing together—"Why Hershey's Kisses love to perform? Because the crowd just eats them up. Little Hershey's Kisses. Big chocolate taste."*
- *A single Kiss in a series of outlandish wraps—"Why are Hershey's Kisses wrapped in foil? Because everything else looks ridiculous. Little Hershey's Kisses. Big chocolate taste."*

A company's logo is an obvious campaign link.

Ads show doll characters in real situations wearing or using cotton fabrics. Headlines start with the Cotton Inc. puff-ball logo.

- *"goodnight"—wearing pajamas*
- *"snuggle"—two pairs of bare feet poking out the bottom of a sheet*
- *"up"—a woman in business casual clothes in an elevator*
- *"warm"—a woman in a winter scene with a turtle-neck sweater*

And there's nothing like using the package, as Absolut vodka does in playing variations on its bottle shape.

Spokespeople can be effective campaign links. Jerry Seinfeld speaks for American Express, Bob Dole for Viagra, Ralph Lauren for Polo, Charles Schwab for the company bearing his name.

Created characters like Ronald McDonald (McDonald's) are enduring. Animated characters like the Pillsbury Doughboy have long lifetimes, as do kid-appeal characters like Tony the Tiger for Kellogg's Frosted Flakes and the Flintstones for Pebbles cereal. Some animal symbols—Morris the Cat for 9-Lives cat food and Budweiser's Clydesdale horses—have been around for decades. AFLAC's quacking duck seems destined for a long run.

The Exxon tiger, introduced by the company (then Esso) in 1964, with the line "Rely on the tiger," later evolved into "Put a tiger in your tank." Some years later, the tiger helped bridge the name change to Exxon with "We've changed our name but not our stripes."

Visual campaign links like these hold campaigns together.

Verbal Similarity

A catchy phrase isn't enough to make a campaign. Many campaign taglines are just that—words at the end of the commercial or print ad that are too often throwaways and could be connected to any brand. Many others only have life and meaning after investment over time. By themselves on a piece of paper, they may not leap out as enduring.

The proper objective is a set of words that illuminates the advertising, encapsulates the message, and can be associated with one brand only:

"Visine gets the red out"

"For all you do, this Bud's for you" (Budweiser)

"Melts in your mouth, not in your hand" (M&M)

"Fly the friendly skies of United"

"The best thing about waking up is Folger's in your cup"

"It's ability, not disability, that counts" (The National Organization on Disability)

A distinctive sound can help make a promise sink in, like Campbell Soup's "Mmm-mmm, good," a forty-year-old promise that gets revived periodically. Also, "[Ding-Dong] Avon Calling" or the NBC chimes.

Some of the best slogans, such as BMW's "The Ultimate Driving Machine," started as headlines. One often hears "We need a tagline to put on coffee mugs for sales meetings." Better to seek headlines rather than taglines.

Similarity of Attitude

Some great campaigns have no single campaign visual and no traditional theme line—or didn't have one when the campaigns were launched. What they have is a consistent point of view about what the brand stands for.

Hershey's first-ever campaign, "The All-American Candy Bar," showed children smiling as they enjoyed a Hershey bar. Its latest uses the promise, "Put a smile on your face."

 All great campaigns have a consistent attitude toward the product and the people who use it. However, similarity of attitude alone is a fragile underpinning for a campaign. It needs to be done strongly, consistently—and well.

GLOBAL CAMPAIGNS

Campaigns that build brands and businesses are founded on big ideas, ideas integrated into all sales communications—everywhere. The growth of global marketing is a result of more open markets, international travel, and communications. Cultural phenomena like popular music, rock stars, and movies are making this easier—entertainment is a global language. China is experiencing an invasion of Pizza Hut, McDonald's, and Kentucky Fried Chicken, Coca-Cola and Esprit and American SUVs.

Even before the internet, international media fueled this trend with satellite television, CNN (seen in 94 countries) and MTV (reaching 100 million viewers). The World Cup soccer finals were watched by three *billion* viewers. ESPN is a global brand.

Moving Ideas Across Borders

Success in global marketing stems from a product or positioning that is relevant to consumer needs. Those needs often vary by culture.

Some products are not highly culture bound and are easier to market around the world—computers or consumer electronics, for example. Foods are more difficult—the closer a particular food comes to being part of one country's staple diet, the harder it is to transfer across borders. Impulse products like ice cream bars are easier to market globally. Some products have to be modified to compete locally, like adding beer to the McDonald's menu in Germany.

While cultures and habits vary, people's emotions are remarkably similar.

Greeting cards address human emotions, and Hallmark markets thousands of them. In a test of relative appeals, the top ten cards in the U.S. were identical to the top ten in England and, with one exception, in the same rank order.

People are very much alike in their attitudes regarding love, hate, fear, greed, envy, joy, patriotism, material comforts, and family. The way in which we touch these emotions may differ from country to country. Britons, for example, tend to be embarrassed by overt emotional appeals, whereas Americans and Australians aren't.

Unlike the unabashed AT&T "Reach out and touch someone" campaign in the U.S., British Telecom used humor to promote phone calls.

Some groups share cross-cultural identities more than others. "Japanese engineers or German teenagers are not foreigners," Peter Drucker observes. "They have the same tastes, values and buying habits as American engineers or American teenagers."

A strong visual helps move ideas around the world.

Dove's antiperspirant campaign moves around the world with symbolic photos in front of a woman's underarm—hot red peppers, dry cracked desert soil, even tennis balls.

"We want the clout that comes with global brands and the relative intimacy the strongest local brands have," says Unilever North American Chairman Charles Strauss.

We have long since moved beyond the naïveté of shipping a commercial around the world with literal translations. That view has been replaced by the understanding that true global campaigns are based on an international (or regional) brand image and strategy—and a local understanding of national language, values, and culture.

First, there is the language barrier. "Come alive with the Pepsi Generation" becomes "Pepsi brings your ancestors back from the grave" in the Chinese translation.

Then there are cultural subtleties. An American Express commercial showing a father putting his arm around his injured daughter was changed in Thailand to show him patting her head.

Brand strategies can and do move worldwide, but it's usually best to create advertising locally from a worldwide plan and strategy—developed with all interested parties. Each country must agree to create advertising on the approved strategy to maintain a consistent brand image. If there is a local market reason to vary strategy, that should be discussed before creative work begins.

Usually there is a single campaign that has been proven in other markets. That's where creative work begins—with a great translation of the campaign into local visuals and language. If the agency comes up with a different campaign, that can be tested against the standard. But the burden of proof is on the challenger.

Most significantly, there must also be a shared advertiser-agency commitment to a global brand. The agency cannot do it alone.

EVOLVING A CAMPAIGN—THE IBM STORY

Solutions for a Small Planet

In mid-1994, the IBM brand was in a harrowing decline. Industry and business press blasted the company for falling behind the times. The publicity was particularly damaging in a technology market comprised of younger, fast-growing niche competitors.

The management of the IBM brand had become increasingly fragmented and its advertising programs, more than two hundred worldwide, became a clear reflection of the problem. The first step in creating a more unified and effective presentation of the brand was to select a single agency partner chartered with brand stewardship for IBM worldwide. IBM charged Ogilvy & Mather with assignments previously handled by forty advertising agencies.

To revitalize the IBM brand, the agency aimed to craft a solution that would create the perception that IBM was truly changing—and to do it on a global basis.

The first charge was to begin to alter perceptions that IBM was for big business only, that their proprietary systems didn't work with non-IBM systems, and that the company was difficult to do business with. The advertising sought to repair the emotional fabric of the brand by creating a new personality for IBM, overcoming its stodgy, tired, and distant personality ("white men in white shirts") with one that was surprising, approachable, human, vigorous, and trustworthy. It aimed to retain and reinforce latent perceived strengths of IBM global technology leadership, quality, reliability, and service.

The creative strategy was to present IBM in a manner that would leverage long-held strengths, like global reach and resources, but reverse the negative feelings people had about the brand. The creative concept introduced an interesting array of people around the world speaking about IBM in their own subtitled languages. The characters in the spots made the message more engaging—and IBM more accessible and appealing.

From Czech nuns "dying to surf the net" to elderly French gentlemen conversing about IBM's laser storage technology, unexpected scenarios allowed these people to talk about IBM in a credible but entertaining manner. The scenarios also positioned IBM at the center of a major shift taking place globally—technology changing how people worked, played, and learned.

The campaign introduced the line "Solutions for a small planet"—an articulation of the message that IBM delivers solutions that are both simple and powerful enough to manage information anywhere, anytime, and for anyone.

The "Subtitles" campaign ran in forty-seven countries and twenty-six languages in every major region of the world. The campaign was designed for global adaptation—it showed people speaking foreign languages, subtitled in the local language. Local markets needed only to change the subtitles. "Subtitles" was a global campaign that embraced all of IBM, an important factor at that tenuous time.

By 1995, *Financial World* rated IBM the third most valuable brand—up from its #282 position the prior year. The rejuvenation of the IBM brand was underway

e-business

The term *e-business* and the signature red e-mark were created in 1997 to help position IBM as the preeminent provider of internet business solutions.

The advertising objective was to educate constituents about the opportunities and benefits of e-business and to interest them in partnering with IBM. The challenge was to do so in a manner that was relevant to business and Information Technology decision makers in countries known for IT innovation, as well as those that had just begun to implement basic PC technology.

Since the launch of the campaign, e-business has acted as an organizing principle for all IBM marketing communications. It serves as a vehicle for communicating brand values and solutions-oriented messages. The e-business principle helps unite communications across IBM's numerous business divisions in more than thirty-five countries.

The message is delivered via a full 360-degree marketing effort in television (to define the opportunities), print (to explain in depth), the web (to demonstrate), outdoor (visibility), direct mail (high-value targets), and events (e-business "live").

The campaign was launched in the U.S. with an intrusive TV teaser which posed the question, "What is an e-business?" and pointed viewers to a blockbuster eight-page insert in *The Wall Street Journal*. The insert explained the vision and provided information on IBM's ability to help businesses become e-businesses.

Other elements of the campaign were rolled out in TV, print, and web banners to demonstrate that e-business is a reality by showing real companies reaping real business benefits. As the campaign expanded beyond the U.S., the work was adapted to ensure local relevance.

- In the U.S.—*www.motorola.com* and *www.nationalgeographic.com*.
- In Japan—*www.yamaha.com*.
- In France—*www. galeriegaultier.com*.
- In Australia—*www.sydney.olympic.org*.

Creative concepts are adapted intelligently rather than translated literally.

A U.S. TV spot called "Chain Reaction" humorously illustrates the challenges of supply chain management by showing a retailer calling her wholesaler to ask, "Where are my socks?" The answer: "Down by the docks." The response: "I've checked every box, but there's no box full of socks." And so on.

A direct translation didn't work in Japan, nor did the technique of rhyming. To get the supply chain message across, the Japanese spot pokes fun at the sharp contrast between the overly deferential treatment of customers and the harsh way one deals with suppliers.

E-business has become part of the vernacular, IBM revenues are growing, brand attitudes are improving, and the world is seeing IBM as a leader in the internet area.

"We have to market effectively on a global basis," says Maureen McGuire, VP for Worldwide Integrated Marketing Communications, "so global campaign planning has been a crucial part of the IBM brand's rejuvenation and ongoing vitality."

We balance unified global strategies with highly relevant local executions. We try to relate to the customers on their terms, in their world. We always look at it from the customers' point of view—what they actually see in their own marketplace.

When to Change Campaigns

Even the most successful campaigns need to be refreshed over time. People change, products change, markets change. Preserving a campaign reverently is one way to lose it.

There are times when campaigns wear out, in the sense that the market has changed so much that a new message is needed.

Advertisers are prone to change campaigns when deeper issues are causing the problem—wrong pricing, outworn product, poor distribution. Change in these circumstances makes the situation worse by giving away the brand equity as well as the delay in dealing with the real issues.

Campaigns often get discarded before they reach their full potential. One research study indicated that the average campaign lasts only seventeen months. The same study showed many campaigns still building awareness and sales after three and four years.

Before you replace a proven campaign with something "better," try to evolve what has worked. If a new campaign falls short, swallow your pride and go back to the proven one before launching yet another effort that will confuse everyone.

5 Media Strategies and Tactics

An explosion of media! How else to describe the proliferation of options in broadcast and print, nontraditional media, new media, media buying services, plus the fragmentation of markets and fractionating of audiences . . . all with a heavy dose of technology and consumer behavior models?

Media is a continually evolving animal, changing on the surface yet still presenting us with questions that stubbornly persist.

- Where should you place your message?
- How often should it run—and for how long?
- How much should you spend?

Every new medium—from radio to television and now the internet—has prompted a fresh look at these questions. Some media pros suggest the media plan should be written *first,* before starting creative work—to make the best use of options to communicate with an audience, rather than with a TV commercial "adapted" to other media.

Wherever one starts, with the media plan or the creative work, all these changes make it possible to target messages more sharply than ever before.

To read a media plan, you must understand media language—and recognize a fundamental truth:

> **Advertising messages carried by the media are not necessarily absorbed by their audiences.**

Viewers may leave the room or just not notice a TV commercial. Magazine readers can just turn the page. So in reality, the measured media audience is not the true measure of reaching the prospect. It is merely the *opportunity* to communicate.

Basic Concepts

Cost per thousand (CPM) is the cost of reaching one thousand things, whether households or women or left-handed golfers. CPM is used to compare the relative efficiency of different media.

> *If a television spot costs $100,000 and reaches 20 million homes, the CPM is $5 ($100,000 divided by 20,000).*

Always ask, "Cost per thousand *what?*"

Reach is the number of different things that have the opportunity to be exposed to a message at least once. It is also known as unduplicated or net audience or "cume."

> *A plan that gets to four out of five homes has a reach of 80.*

Frequency is the number of times the message is potentially seen or heard in a defined period of time. It is usually expressed as an average. Reach and frequency are measured together over the same time period, commonly four weeks.

Frequency distribution deals with the exact number of times individuals are exposed to advertising in a schedule.

Heavy viewers might be reached with a frequency of 12, light viewers with only one or two exposures.

Impressions represent the total number of messages delivered by a media plan, whatever the medium used—the number of people who have the opportunity to see at least one message multiplied by the number of times they see it.

"Share of voice" is a brand's percent of impressions in a category compared to its competitors.

Broadcast Concepts

Rating is the percent of homes or individuals tuned to the program. It's often reported on an average quarter-hour basis.

If one out of five homes are tuned to a program, it has a 20 rating.

Gross rating points (GRP) is the total of all rating points achieved for a specific schedule or campaign.

A plan with three 20-rated spots delivers 60 GRPs.

Plans calling for selectivity contain terms like WGRPs, for "women GRPs."

How to Use Reach and Frequency

First, recognize that reach and frequency are interrelated. At a given rating level, as reach goes up, frequency goes down. You can't have both unless you add more rating points.

The relationship between reach, frequency, and rating points is expressed in the formula R × F = GRP.

A plan that delivers a 90 reach and a frequency of four produces 360 GRPs in a four-week period (or 90 per week).

The issue is whether the plan can achieve the goals of the strategy. If your objective is to get 50 percent of homes to be aware of your product, it cannot be done if reach is less than 50 percent.

CONTINUITY—THE KEY TO SUCCESS

Most advertising success stories are ones of continuity rather than impact.

This fundamental principle derives from the fact that people's memories are short, a finding first reported by German psychologist Hermann Ebbinghaus in 1885, and since confirmed in other studies.

What the professor discovered was that:

- *People forget 60 percent of what they learn within a half-day.*
- *The more repetition, the more retention.*
- *Forgetting is rapid immediately after learning, then levels off.*

People don't pay attention to advertising—and they forget quickly.

Repetition Aids Retention

Advertisers who seek to reach a broad audience at the expense of sufficient continuity among key prospects risk wasting much of their investment.

For a product that is purchased frequently (soap or toothpaste, for example), the need for "reminder" advertising is obvious. It is also important to register the message for products purchased occasionally.

A case may be made for impact—concentrating everything in a dramatic program that rises above the clutter and commands attention. It is a risky concept that relies on the *hope* that people will remember.

 The dilemma is how to stretch advertising dollars to reach enough people with sufficient continuity. Ideally, it would be great to advertise for 52 weeks. Since that isn't practical for most advertisers, compromises between effective levels and budgets, such as flighting and pulsing, have been used over the years.

The most current research suggests that it is more effective to advertise continuously—even a single occasional spot, than to schedule heavy bursts of advertising followed by long periods of no advertising.

Since 52-week schedules are generally unrealistic, it is better to stretch the advertising periods than to be out entirely (providing an opportunity to a competitor). At the same time, there are instances—special promotional periods, new product introductions, announcements—when it makes sense to heavy up, even if it means cutting back weeks of advertising.

There is no perfect media plan. Given the choice between four four-week flights of advertising at a given level against eight flights at lower levels, the latter is probably better.

The case for repetition is made by *The Wall Street Journal* in its own trade campaign.

> *Study after study has proven conclusively that the more people are exposed to your advertising, the more they will like your product and buy your product. Furthermore, the value of repetition is cumulative, which means that far too often advertising is pulled just as it's beginning to work.*

The *Journal* cites studies by the Advertising Research Foundation and the Association of Business Publishers, by Alfred Politz Media Studies and by W. R. Simmons & Associates Research, and concludes:

It's clear that creating a strong message is only a start. The more you repeat it, the stronger it gets.

The Value of "Recency"

Recency is the payoff of continuity. Studies of product usage data combined with exposure to advertising show:

The most valuable message is the last one before the decision to buy.

"Optimizers"—media models that allow media planners to examine schedules against goals such as Reach, Frequency, and levels of advertising—help stretch budgets. Understanding the value of Recency gives planners another tool to set appropriate goals.

A frequency of one exposure per week may provide reasonable continuity, but two or three per week is less valuable than spreading the exposures over several weeks. The exposure on Week 3 is not as valuable as an exposure on Week 4—if the purchase decision is made after the exposure on Week 4.

Whatever the timing, it is risky to be out of advertising for long periods of time.

FISH WHERE THE FISH ARE

Put your money where your business is—or where you want it to be. Media planning starts with a statement of objectives.

Who Do You Want to Reach?

Describe your audience's demographics—their age, sex, income, education, family status—and buying habits.

Be precise. Not "primary emphasis on men" but "70 percent of messages to men, 30 percent to women."

Describe their lifestyle or "psychographics."

Translate descriptions into actionable terms. Not "influentials" but "chief executive officers" or "directors of cultural institutions."

Describe how the decision process works.

Families are the best customers for fast food restaurants. Parents make the decision to eat out and determine a bank of acceptable restaurants for the occasion. The child usually selects which one from that group—hence, Ronald McDonald.

When Do You Want to Reach Them?

Do people buy your product year-round, or primarily in the summer or on weekends or just when it rains? Some products are keyed to holidays—candy around Halloween, barbecue sauce for July Fourth.

Be specific. What percent of messages should be allocated by quarter, by month, or even by day of week or time of day?

Allocate your media to periods when people decide to buy, not necessarily when they make the purchase.

The higher the price tag, the longer the lead time. Travel to Europe peaks in summer—the decision is made in spring.

Where Do They Live?

All business is local and varies across the country. National marketers face a tough decision—whether to advertise nationally or locally.

Be specific when describing key markets and what percent of business they represent. Total sales may be higher in a large market like New York, but Bostonians may be better customers.

How Do You Want to Reach Them?
What is the best environment for the prospect—and the advertising?

Products have different growth curves.

- *New packaged goods products typically aim for high trial during the initial months, then try to sustain this level with repeat purchases.*
- *People don't buy cold medicines until they have a cold. Awareness builds rapidly, but sales growth is slower. The same is true of dog foods—dog owners tend not to switch brands until the dog stops eating what is in the bowl.*

What other points should the media planner consider?

HOW TO GET BETTER MEDIA PLANS

1. Agree in advance on media objectives and strategies. Make sure you understand the implications of the need for impact or continuity, minimum reach or frequency goals, the values assigned to different magazines, and so on. Goals must be consistent with and derived from the overall marketing plan.

2. Integrate the creative work into planning. Creative and media plans each start from the same strategic premise, but are then executed on separate tracks. It is crucial that there is a working relationship between the two disciplines to secure the best environment for the message.

Should there be different campaigns for different media if a campaign doesn't work well in the recommended medium? Not if the audience is the same. A good campaign has a memorable idea and should be able to translate to most media.

3. Look beyond the obvious. Do you need the visual impact of TV, or can you use a more selective medium?

Do you need full pages in print, or can you use smaller units and run them more frequently? (Same with color—is it functional or decorative?)

4. Look beyond cost per thousand. CPM can be oversimplified as an evaluation tool. It is a starting point, but only measures cost—not effectiveness.

5. Think about clutter. Short message lengths stretch media dollars. They build frequency with fewer dollars. The average 15-second spot is two-thirds as effective as a 30-second spot—at only half the cost.

While shorter message lengths look good in a media plan, they reduce the effectiveness of all advertising through clutter. A 15-second commercial can do a lot of things for a brand, but not everything.

6. Recognize that all media plans are a compromise. The goal is to achieve a balance among options—reach, frequency, weeks of advertising, geography . . . and budget. Don't expect simple answers.

7. Balance local and national need. Network television delivers its audience unevenly across the country and may be underdelivering in some of your key markets. The media plan will have to compensate with spot television, particularly in key markets.

The same is true for print. Magazines deliver differently from area to area.

8. Evaluate alternate plans. The best way to determine how well the plan meets the objectives is to look at several tactical alternatives. Since a media plan is highly quantifiable, it's easy to check it against the specific objectives set for it.

9. Tie the plan closely to marketing goals. If the brand's objective is to maintain market position, allocate spending where the brand's sales are high expressed as a percentage of population—a *brand development index (BDI)*.

To expand and grow in new markets, consider an allocation based on where the brand is weak but other brands sell well—a *category development index (CDI)*.

10. Be creative. Consider product samples tipped in magazines, special programs developed for your audience, bus stop shelters with messages for local neighborhoods.

Or pay to have your product used in a movie, TV program, or video game. "Product integration" (or product placement) has moved beyond making a deal showing a product in a TV program or movie to "virtual" product integration—electronically grafting a sponsor's name behind home plate in a baseball game or placing the Target Stores bull's-eye logo onto a crate in "Survivor." You can't zap these ads because they're part of the show.

HOW MUCH TO SPEND ON ADVERTISING?

> *"What's the most important reason to advertise this year?" The answer: "Next year."*

Whether advertising is viewed as an expense or an investment, the pragmatic response is:

> **Be prepared to *invest* whatever is required to do the job.**
>
> **Better to stay home and not advertise than to invest too little.**

There are computer models that theorize a relationship between profitability, market share, and media spending, but they require detailed historical data and validation in the marketplace.

Short of that, there are business analysis techniques a media planner can use to gauge how much to spend.

- How much is competition spending?
- What is their market share—and share of voice?
- What is your market-share goal?
- How much must you invest to have a share of voice equal to your share of market?
- What are your basic requirements for coverage, frequency, and weeks of advertising?
- Are there standards for advertising-to-sales ratios or cost per unit of sales?

For a new product, the spending level is part of the test plan. Alternate spending levels can be tested.

Test in at least two markets. Test at least a 50 percent increase in spending—anything smaller is too small to read.

For an established product, continually test how far is up. Try higher spending levels, new media, new markets. If you're fortunate enough to have a brand that is successful, it's wise to have a spending test in the market at all times. If it works, roll it out and start another test.

One of the interesting questions advertisers face is whether to concentrate all efforts on a single umbrella brand or to segment efforts into targeted "sub-brands." Since targeted messages are generally more effective, that has to be balanced with the economies of promoting one brand. The general principle is to avoid sub-brands until they are large enough to sustain their own media budgets.

The ultimate issues are accountability and return-on-investment.

Advertising helped create the Midas Muffler brand during its tremendous growth in the 1990s, says Ken Olshan, former Chairman of Wells Rich Green. Here's how he described the Midas spending formula of that time.

> *Under the Midas budget approach, franchisees contribute 5 percent of sales to a national advertising fund every year. The annual 5 percent is policy; it's in the franchise agreement. While I do not advocate spending a flat percentage of sales, because it is not sensitive to market conditions—there is wisdom to be gained from the Midas experience.*
>
> *Midas' big idea is* constancy. *For more than three decades, Midas' marketing people and advertising agencies have known that they have 5 percent of sales to work with—never more, never less. They can't ask for more, and they don't give anything back at the end of the year.*

Olshan goes on to describe how Midas measures ROI.

> *Midas tracks weekly the number of jobs completed for mufflers, brakes, shocks, and such. They also measure brand awareness and customer attitudes. Then, they measure these results against their advertising and promotion schedules so they can gauge what is working and what isn't.*
>
> *Finally, Midas compares year-to-year sales at the national, regional, market and single-shop levels. Since 5 percent is a constant from year to year, they have historical data to help them evaluate the media mix, the product mix, and the creative approach.*
>
> *Ultimately, the dealers are the stakeholders who contribute 5 percent of their hard-won money. Like shareholders, they expect to get value for their investment.*

 The drive to accountability is echoed by Publicis Group Chairman Maurice Levy, saying to the American Association of Advertising Agencies: "I believe that every client's obligation is to be very specific about the terms of success, and every agency's duty is to challenge that objective and plan to it."

NONTRADITIONAL MEDIA

Clutter on television—the time devoted to nonprogramming content like commercials and promotions—continues to increase. Now up to 18 minutes each hour in some time periods, clutter makes viewers less likely to watch or remember ads.

With ad-skipping devices also growing, how does the advertiser break through? Add the decline of mass media, the rise of cable TV, special-interest magazines, new media devices, digital files of music and films, shelves filled with videotapes and other distractions at home, and the target becomes more elusive.

All this leads advertisers to explore ads on supermarket shopping carts, airline in-flight videos, ski lifts, taxicab roofs (and back seats), or restaurant ads on maps. The media world reinvents itself so rapidly that it is important to keep a sensible perspective. Don't get carried away with new technologies and predictions about the demise of some media, but be open to nontraditional media opportunities.

Word-of-mouth has always been considered the best advertising of all, Malcolm Gladwell points out in his book *The Tipping Point*. He writes:

> *Think, for a moment about the last expensive restaurant you went to, the last expensive piece of clothing you bought, and the last movie you saw. In how many of those cases was your decision about where to spend your money influenced by the*

recommendation of a friend? There are plenty of advertising executives who think that precisely because of the sheer ubiquity of marketing efforts these days, word-of-mouth appeals have become the only kind of persuasion that most of us respond to anymore.

Gladwell cites Hush Puppies, the brushed-suede shoes with the lightweight crepe sole, which went from being out of fashion to a hip fashion statement and then to every mall in America on the strength of word-of-mouth—"buzz"—that started among kids in New York's East Village and SoHo.

Word-of-mouth can be engineered.

Henry Weinhard's Private Reserve, the best-selling super-premium beer in the Northwest, was launched without conventional advertising but by word-of-mouth.

"Henry's" was introduced at selected bars, and the bartender was made an insider with a fact sheet talking about the extra hops and slow brewing time. Only after the word started to spread was it distributed in limited stores, and only when its reputation had grown was it introduced into supermarkets—with quirky advertising that created yet more word-of-mouth.

In the world of the internet, word-of-mouth is *viral marketing.*

Before any advertising ran, Alka-Seltzer Morning Relief (a line extension) was launched with internet messages to party planners, disk jockeys, restaurateurs, bartenders—to create buzz among people who might be in a position to recommend hangover relief.

Viral marketing starts with the question: "What do my consumers do for fun, and how can my brand play with them?" Advergames—branded games that act as commercials—do more than sell products. They build relationships with individual consumers via two-way dialogues, and demonstrate the codependence of broadcast, cable, and online media.

"Guerrilla marketing" (or "stealth marketing") employs tactics like hiring actors to use your product in public, drawing a logo in the sand on a beach, or spray-painting the Linux icon, the penguin, along with symbols for peace and love on the streets of major cities. It appealed to the rebel nature of the audience with the line "Peace Love Linux." Microsoft placed its butterfly logo on streets, buildings, and posts in New York City to introduce MSN 8 internet service. They were forced to remove the decals (which adhered with friction) and apologize, but the point was made.

> *The Wow Factory, a new agency dedicated to bringing "buzz" into campaigns, uses nontraditional tactics such as people carrying TV monitors, a modern version of the sandwich board.*

And this doesn't include product publicity and other ideas for free media. In addition to the familiar press release, there is the Video News Release—essentially a press release (with legitimate news or feature value) placed in TV newscasts and on internet news sites.

Nontraditional media provide attractive opportunities, but can't do the job on their own. It's best to use them selectively, since they are neither measurable nor accountable. In any case, there will always be many traditional media around and available.

Integrating Creative and Media

The emergence of giant independent planning and buying services has made it more difficult to integrate media with the strategic and creative functions, a strange development in a business where global consolidation and message integration are getting more important. The media companies counter by claiming (in addition to lower costs) advertisers get more objective "media neutral" solutions.

Clearly, not all messages are equal—some are far more effective than others. Chasing rating points or efficiency alone is not an answer. At some point in the process, creative and media planning must be brought together.

6 Target Marketing

Every generation gets a label—Baby Boomers, Generation X, Generation Y, and so on. The 2000 Census reports the growth of Hispanics, Asians, and other new demographics. Research adds insights into attitudinal segments. And we recognize differences in marketing to women, children, and senior citizens.

Whether they know it or not, each of these is a target.

With more data on consumers and their habits and preferences, plus segmented media and databases, precision marketing is the order of the day. For many products and services, there will always be a need for mass audiences. For smaller, more defined segments or even individuals, there is less reason to use mass media and more opportunity to deliver a personalized message.

> *The basic idea behind customer segmentation is that communications are most effective when highly targeted. Not only do different audiences respond better to different messages and different tones of voice, but a company's communications objectives may also vary by audience.*
>
> —OGILVY & MATHER WORLDWIDE

There are several ways to slice the consumer pie.

Demographics are a starting point. Gender, age, race, income, family size, and education tell us a lot about the consumer target. Census 2000 confirmed that the U.S. population is older, more ethnically diverse, and increasingly living in nontraditional families—single parents, unmarried couples, or divorced or never-married individuals.

Following the disputed 2000 presidential election, *Brandweek* magazine made the case there are two Americas—red states (votes that went Republican) and blue (Democrat) states. More than political differences, their analysis shows a range of cultural and attitudinal differences.

> *This election was Hollywood vs. Nashville, Sex and the City vs. Touched by an Angel, National Public Radio vs. Talk Radio.*
>
> —JOURNALIST TERRY MATTINGLY

New segmentations, based on people's attitudes toward issues and products, are constantly emerging.

Coming of Age

Put together age and attitudes, and you get the shared values of a generation. Making the case for "cohort marketing" in their book *Defining Markets, Defining Moments*, Geoffrey Meredith and Charles Schewe write about the latent feelings and values formed when people come of age.

> *. . . a time that for most of us falls roughly between the ages of 17 and 23. While in this age span, your customers likely fell in love for the first time, became economic beings, developed their own value systems, explored new ideas, and essentially,*

 became adults. Coming of age is a very powerful time, and the values instilled then last a lifetime.

In the 1920s, there was Scott Fitzgerald's "Lost Generation." In the 1950s, it was the "Silent Generation." In the 1980s, there was the "Yuppie Generation." Now we have "Generation X," the group of people born between 1961 and 1981, described as Xers because they represent something negative to their elders. "Generation Y" people were born between 1979 and 1994, the sons and daughters of "Baby Boomers"—more racially diverse, more computer literate, more aware of brands . . . and very different from GenX. Each was influenced by events of the time.

Labels change; the principle of understanding shared experiences and attitudes remains.

The New Achievers

Technology has created a new kind of blue-collar worker, the electronic blue-collar worker. The fastest-growing well-paid occupations in the U.S. are computer operators, medical assistants, electronics technicians, and other "electric blues."

For these groups, experience becomes more important than possessions. Symbols of the good life, like the BMW or the swimming pool, give way to indulgences like travel and home services.

The Time Seekers

As society becomes more affluent, its time becomes more precious. Studies show that fewer Americans feel they have enough leisure time—particularly families with two working parents. More people are making tough choices between more money and more time.

People are now saying they are willing to give up current income for leisure time, and that is a big

> *change," observes an economics professor at Harvard. "A shift in materialistic values is taking place.*

Increasingly, people will pay a premium for goods and services that buy them time—cell phones, dog walkers, lawn care services, and home shopping by phone or web site.

Life Simplifiers

The proliferation of choices in consumer goods, technologies, and media creates a whirl of confusion and stress. Too much choice leads to services that help consumers make the right one—TV and movie critics to help decide what to watch, fashion consultants in stores, consumer reports on products, even people to help organize your closet.

Branded products and services bring the added value of simplification through the assurance of quality and reliability.

> *Consumers like brands because they package meaning," says Alex Biel, former head of the Ogilvy Center for Research and Development. "They form a kind of shorthand that makes choice easier. They let me escape from a feature-by-feature analysis of category alternatives.*

Premium Brand Consumers

In almost all product categories, premium brands emerge—often followed by super-premium brands. Once the province of just the well-to-do, premium products are now for *everyone*. Consider the plumber or landscaper who spends winter vacations in Aspen or the Caribbean islands, or the dental assistant with the Gucci bag or Hermès scarf.

Premium brands start with quality, not snob appeal, and a carefully crafted marketing program that creates "specialness." It is crucial to understand the psychology of what people look for in a premium product. Selling prestige is a fast way to fail. Understatement is a better strategy.

DEMOGRAPHIC SEGMENTS

Asian-Americans, Hispanics, and African-Americans are the major growth segments in the U.S. By the year 2005, ethnic Americans will represent one in three Americans. By 2040, they will account for half the country's population.

Four other segments—women, children, seniors, gays and lesbians—also require special consideration in advertising.

Hispanics

The Hispanic community has emerged as the largest and fastest-growing market, up to more than 13 percent of the population. It's concentrated in large cities in three regions—the Mexican-American population in the Southwest and southern California, the Cuban community in southern Florida, and the Puerto Rican and Caribbean communities in New York, the Northeast, and Chicago.

Accents and speech patterns vary, and there is enormous cultural diversity from twenty countries of origin, but all Hispanics use the same Spanish language dictionary.

> *The futurists are right when they predict that the U.S. is becoming a bilingual country, with Spanish being the second language.*
>
> —HECTOR ORCI, LA AGENCIA DE ORCI Y ASOCIADOS

Local merchants—car dealers, furniture stores, doctors, lawyers—were first to discover the need to communicate to this market in its first language, Spanish, and the payoff in doing so. They were followed by virtually every major advertiser (and politician). Today, some $2 billion is spent in Spanish media, PR, and promotions to pursue the over 35 million Hispanics in the U.S. with the purchasing power of $450 billion.

Several cosmetics companies now acknowledge the growing nonwhite population with products for darker skins, and advertise them in Spanish as well as English.

> *Hispanic networks have done a great job marketing themselves by saying, 'These are the demographics who buy your clients' products, and in some instances they are more important than the general market' because many Latino families tend to be younger and larger than other American families.*
>
> —JOE MANDESE, *MEDIA BUYER'S DAILY*

Hispanics are reached efficiently by two major Spanish-language TV networks, Univision and Telemundo. They watch TV and listen to radio more than they buy newspapers or magazines. They also represent the largest segment of new web users.

They respond best, says Hispanic agency head Lionel Sosa, to "carefully crafted, culturally relevant messages that touch on the values they hold dear, while depicting them as Americans, not a separate group."

Asian-Americans

> *Every morning, Jing Xu reads five newspapers. Of the five, only one is in English. The others are in Chinese. 'The English media just doesn't cover all the news I'm interested in,' says 30-year-old Ms. Xu, who emigrated from China a decade ago and now lives in San Francisco.*
>
> — *THE WALL STREET JOURNAL*

The article goes on to describe the high levels of ethnic-media usage in California, the first "majority minority" state in the mainland U.S.

The Asian-American community speaks many languages—spoken by Chinese (in several dialects), Japanese, Koreans, Vietnamese, Filipinos, plus Indians and Pakistanis from the Asian subcontinent.

It may be difficult to talk to this market, but it is worth the effort. The growth rate alone makes it hard to ignore. Compared to the total U.S. population, Asian-Americans are more affluent and better educated. They are increasingly well represented in management and the professions.

At 12 million people, this is not the smallest community, neither is it as large and homogeneous as others. There is no single, simple communications solution. Avoid trying to talk to everyone at once, and avoid stereotypes (exotic-looking women or dragons). Capture nuances.

African-Americans

Black people are not dark-skinned white people, says Tom Burrell of Burrell Communications. Further:

> *Blacks are significantly different in terms of approach—our history, how we came here, how we developed as citizens. There is a significant difference in behavior, and that manifests itself all the way to the marketplace.*

The first principle of advertising to Blacks—*make it believable*. It's the little things that make a difference. The casting, the language, what actors are wearing in a commercial can make the difference between one that hits home or is a turnoff.

The second principle—*don't insult people's intelligence.*

Don't patronize; avoid stereotypes. An all-white commercial in Black media is not just missing a business opportunity—it is insulting. A single Black actor or actress in an otherwise all-white commercial is obvious tokenism. Situations that are not part of a Black lifestyle irritate and can backfire.

Women

After the start of the women's movement, it became fashionable to single out women as targets with special marketing devices—hotel rooms fitted in pink and white, special Women's Services Departments in banks. Women refused to stay in those rooms or to stand in line at those banks.

Treat women as consumers. That's what they are.

> *The illustration—a woman's underwear drawer, with panties labeled "Monday, Tuesday, Wednesday, Thursday, Friday, Market Closed, Market Closed." The headline—"Changing the way women think about investing." Other ads in the series for Women & Co., a Citigroup unit, show a stock ticker circling a baby's crib and a* Wall Street Journal *outside a child's plastic play house.*

Women—especially working women—respond to ideas that will save them time. They respond more than men to emotional appeals, but don't single them out in the advertising as irrational airheads. They want to be treated as people, not stereotypes. As one marketer put it, Helen Homemaker is no more an absolute reality than Betty Briefcase.

Children

Marketing to young children is a delicate issue. Children are heavy viewers of television. They watch more *adult* TV than children's programs, according to Nielsen. TV is an especially pervasive medium among children under ten. They buy products with their own money or nag parents to buy things for them.

"Today's kids are no fools and far more sophisticated than they were 20 years ago when many of today's children's advertising guidelines were written," says Jerry McGee, who ran perhaps the largest children's advertising agency. "Those guidelines need to be updated—and consistently applied across all networks. Other media are virtually unmonitored, and anyone knows that it is virtually impossible to monitor kids 24/7 as they multitask their way throughout the day."

McGee notes how computers and media proliferation have changed things. In his words:

> *Kids are incredibly adept at culling information from the media, and they spend countless hours in multimedia searches learning about their favorite brands. This is especially true in the video game world.*
>
> *They also work differently than a generation ago. Instead of sitting at their desk doing their homework, they tend to watch TV, surf the net, listen to music in their earphones all at once. They have learned to multi-process information from several sources at once. Multitasking is standard behavior.*

A survey by NeoPets, a youth-oriented web site, shows that children love the internet—and recognize the main goal of advertising is to make them buy things. "This idea that kids don't know the difference between advertising and content . . . [is] simply not true," says a NeoPets executive.

There are several children's markets (and they differ for boys and girls). Preschoolers rely most on parental decisions. Yet they are becoming very brand aware, getting on the computer, and nagging and influencing their parents for some purchases. The six-to-eight-year-old kids are faddists, and the heaviest viewers of television.

Kid marketer Paul Kurnit says the phenomenon of age compression called KGOY (Kids Are Getting Older Younger) creates new segments such as three-to-eight-year-olds—engaged with toys but checking out of kiddie things earlier. Then come the silver bullet influencers in kid marketing—nine to twelve-year-old "tweens," not kids, not teens.

Children are a special audience, and there are principles of effective communications.

Make the product fun.

Today's food products have to do something more than just taste good. The food industry has been wooing kids with color. Heinz has created green ketchup, complete with a thin nozzle that invites them to make designs on their hamburgers. Chocolate and blue French fries are already on the market, as is blue margarine from Parkay.

Make the product fun, make the advertising funny—the zanier and broader, the better. Kids love slapstick comedy.

> *In the Flintstones campaign for Pebbles cereal, Barney constantly finds inventive ways to trick Fred into giving up his good-tasting cereal. The kids all know what's going to happen—and they love it.*

Funny, says Kurnit, "but not at the expense of the product. Humor must be relevant and elevating of the product as hero." The novelty and appeal of colored foods must be balanced by consumerist and parental concerns about foods that compound obesity problems or confuse children about nutrition.

Children like reality.

They can relate to things that grow out of their own experience—sleep-over parties for girls, hand-clapping games for young children. They like the action and excitement of online reality games.

Create a personality for the product.
It will keep kids loyal, and they won't easily switch.

> *Barbie, the world's largest-selling fashion doll, helps little girls live out their fantasies with aspirational products and advertising. Barbie remains a leader by staying current with contemporary lifestyles—as does her Black counterpart Shani.*

Children love to get mail. Their parents get tons of mail, points out OgilvyOne, but they don't.

> *Barbie realized this years ago and began to write to young girls. Naturally they were excited to be receiving mail from a "friend," especially since each mailing always contained something to paint, to put together, or to play with.*

Music is key.
Music is the single most powerful influence among kids. At all ages, it is a universal language. Kids know the music videos, and they love to dance. Not just kiddie music but contemporary genres like Hip Hop, Reggae, and Rap.

Be careful with casting.
Children emulate older children. When in doubt, cast older (but not out of the age range).

Girls may emulate boys, but boys won't emulate girls. When in doubt, cast boys (at least for unisex products).

Girls are wired differently.
Girls e-mail, boys play computer games. Boys respond best to action and excitement. Both boys and girls respond to kindness and friendship.

Girls prefer commercials with a song, that show lots of kids, and are funny, says the Gepetto Group. Boys like commercials that are action-packed, loud, and funny. Girls today feel they can do it all. "I can do girl stuff and boy stuff. But boys can't do girl stuff."

Children's advertising can be effective *and* socially responsible. The Children's Advertising Review Unit of the Council of Better Business Bureaus is helpful in defining the guidelines for advertising to children.

Senior Citizens

Quick! Do you know the fastest-growing age group in the U.S.? It is people who are going to live to be over 100! There will be some four million of them by the middle of the century.

> *While people age 50 and older account for only 27 percent of the population, they represent nearly 50 percent of total consumer demand [and] will increase with the aging of boomers.*
>
> —KEN DYCHTWALD, FOUNDER, AGE WAVE

They also represent 80 percent of all luxury travel and buy 48 percent of all luxury cars.

Age has become as much a state of mind as it is one of chronology. Today's seniors are nothing like the grandparents of the last generation. They are thinking younger and living longer. They are leading more dynamic lives, often starting second careers. They are healthier and wealthier, with more time to spend their money.

The Center for Mature Studies at Georgia State University segments the elderly into four groups—Healthy Hermits, Ailing Outgoers, Healthy Indulgers, and Frail Reclusives. Ken Dychtwald prefers to segment them according to their stages in life—empty-nesters and grandparents, then (sometimes) single again.

"Old" is often seen as fifteen years older than a person's age—at any point in life. Most of these seniors see themselves as fifteen years younger than their chronological age. *Modern Maturity* features articles on going back to school and how to win at tennis, as well as the expected tips on estate planning.

Advertising that shows seniors as infirm, ill, lonely, or sexless hits the wrong note. Products that meet their needs, like low-sodium foods or Viagra, do well with a vigorous self-portrait in advertising.

The most successful campaigns targeted at mature consumers, says *The Economist*, focus on "active and healthy lifestyles and introduce positive role models. Rejuvenated patients cycling with their grandchildren or practicing *tai chi* are far more effective then the stereotype of a frail arthritic sufferer."

Gays and Lesbians

The gay, lesbian, and transgender population (GLBT) is estimated at anywhere from 11 to 23 million people. Yet no major media or attitudinal research tracking company (such as Nielsen or Simmons) breaks out these consumers. Census questionnaires ask only about household "makeup," not sexual preferences. So the importance of this affluent, trendsetting segment has not been recognized.

Advertisers have recently started to enter this market, making it a more visible and acceptable place to be. Coors, American Airlines, and Seagram's pioneered this market, and have been joined by American Express, IBM, John Hancock, and others.

Turn on your TV set, and you're likely to see a sitcom or drama featuring a gay or lesbian. "Ellen" was one of the first; successes like "Will & Grace" and "Queer as Folks" soon followed.

Go to your newsstand. Gay and lesbian magazines have proliferated. You'll find OUT, The Advocate, Genre, Passport, Curve, *and many others.*

Gay and lesbian celebrities are sought after for endorsements. Tennis star Martina Navratilova appears for Subaru.

Absolut vodka has been a pioneer in marketing to this niche group. Michel Roux, president and CEO of Carillon Importers (the former distributor of Absolut), always said he wanted to court gay men and lesbians because they were trendsetters whose brand preferences would be emulated by younger, hipper segments of the general public.

Even advertisers not targeting the gay market are increasingly showing gay people as a way to stand out and be inclusive. Marketers who want to reach gays and lesbians say advertising is most effective when it speaks to the desire for one-on-one relationships and families.

John Hancock created a commercial showing two women with their adopted Asian child. "You'll make a wonderful mother," one said to the other. "So will you," she replied with a smile.

An engaging commercial for Miller beer targeted gays but also appealed to non-gays.

Two women, cruising a bar for a man, spot one and send him a beer. They're delighted to find he has a handsome friend. Their plans are thwarted when the men take each other's hands. "Well," one of the women sighs, "at least he's not married."

The secret of marketing to gays is the same as that for marketing to any special segment—don't patronize, avoid tokenism, be authentic, believe in what you are doing.

"You can't fake a Corporate Soul," says futurist Faith

 Popcorn. "Either you have one, or you'd better create one, fast."

Precision Marketing

The growing importance of market segments is one of the most powerful trends in American society. Stunning advances in technology and media enable advertisers to talk more directly to individuals or groups in terms of their specific interests. Together, these create a new level of precision in marketing.

7 Integrated Communications

It happens all the time. Consumers visit a web site or talk to a service rep or open a mail package from a brand they think they know and like. And they feel let down. Disappointed. That feeling they had about the brand, that idea lodged in their head, was that "just the advertising?"

Integrating brand strategy down through every "touch point" between the brand and your customer is not just a nicety. Consumers are expert at reading the body language of a brand.

> *Westin Hotels settled on bed and bath as key opportunities to distinguish their brand. Under the headlines "The Heavenly Bed" and "The Heavenly Bath," Westin promised luxury in both—and backed this up with the opportunity to buy their special bed ensemble, mattress, pillows, sham, sheets, blanket, duvet, bed skirt, bathrobe, bath sheet, dual-head shower, curved shower rod, shower curtain, even roller-style shower hooks.*

Every touch point, especially employees.

> *"In service businesses—FedEx promising to deliver your packages overnight, Verizon promising*

 wireless reception anywhere—employees must embrace this promise, and live it."

—TONI MALONEY, MARKETING CONSULTANT

When brand actions don't match brand promises, trust is broken. And trust is what building brands is all about.

THE MULTICHANNEL CONSUMER

More consumers are interacting with more brands in more ways than ever before. They are shopping in catalogs and buying on the web. Or shopping on the web and buying in the store. Or seeing a TV spot that sends them to the phone to ask for a brochure.

Studies show that the more ways consumers interact with a brand, the more they remember the brand and the more they buy.

Brands are built and sustained by unified and consistent messaging in all customer touch points. So how do you keep all these communications—advertising, direct mail, e-mail, web site, telemarketing, promotion, point of sale—consistent in all these media and distribution channels? Who brings it all together—and how?

In broad-based TV and print media, where the goal is to drive awareness of the brand position, the strategy is about how the creative should communicate it. In integrating channels and media, the challenge is to *prove* the truth of the advertising—to turn brand strategy into brand behavior and show that what the brand does is consistent with what the brand says. The strategy is about how the channel or medium itself can bring the brand to life.

Too many people think that the identical brand message should simply be repeated in every medium and channel. What happens then is that all touch points are saying the same thing but none is taking advantage of what each channel can *uniquely* do to prove the strategy and make it real.

If a coffee company says it is European, the integrated strategy is to make every point of contact between the company and the consumer feel "Euro"—telemarketers with accents, packages with several languages, international addresses, etc.

Integration is more than just creative.

Integration is the process of ensuring that everything a brand says and does in every channel is aligned with what the brand promises. To achieve it, look at integration on three levels.

1. Strategically

Every program and communication should be a natural outgrowth of the brand strategy.

Tide stands for the best way to clean and care for clothes. The brand has stayed true to that in everything from commercials (featuring testimonials from L.L.Bean and other makers of quality clothes) to their web site, "The Tide Fabric Care Network."

Clairol repositioned its brand to stand for "A Beauty All Your Own," and examined everything that touched the customer. A new promotion invited women to write in "your idea of beauty." The web site and e-mails provided online tools that allowed women to try different hair colors on their scanned photographs. The customer newsletter was personalized with offers and information tailored for each customer. All touch points offered ways for consumers to register and provide their names for the database.

2. Programmatically

All elements in the media and channel mix should work together as part of the customer experience. If you send a direct-mail letter with a free offer, make sure you don't send an e-mail with a different offer at the same time.

Program integration simply means that when you provide a phone number in an ad, the phone will be answered by somebody who knows what the ad is about. And when you provide a web address, the landing page will have the information you should expect. The content is coordinated at every point.

3. Creatively

All communications in all channels and media should have a consistent look and feel.

The objective of the United States Postal Service's web site was to reach a wide range of different targets for its Priority Mail service. TV and print raised overall awareness and drove people to the web site. Direct mail and e-mail were tailored for each prospect, inviting visitors to the site.

Each communication delivered the message in a way that was relevant to the target and creatively consistent, using the line "What's your e-priority?" A look was developed just for this campaign—bold red and blue graphics plus black and white photos.

A TV commercial opens with a USPS logo and "Fact #7. Packages." The people cite the cost of two-day package delivery: FedEx—$12, UPS—$6, USPS—$3. Other commercials compare delivery costs for Saturdays, trucks, airplanes, and so on, and close with "$12. $6. $3. What's your priority?"

Direct mail pieces use the same graphic treatment and comparative pricing with headlines for each target audience.

- *"Using Priority Mail does more than show your clients how much you care. It also shows you're good at arithmetic."*

- *"You just lost one of your best excuses to get out of the office. Because from now on we'll bring the Post Office to you."*
- *"Not only do we deliver supplies to your door, we offer a very attractive pricing policy. How does free sound?"*

A unified brand image in all media.

START WITH A CORE CONCEPT

The days of starting with a TV commercial and "translating" it to other media are fading. Increasingly, we're starting with a core concept of the brand developed and agreed to by all parties. This must be boiled down to a few words succinct enough that everyone working on the program can remember them—what former Nike marketing chief Scott Bedbury calls a "mantra." Nike's core concept is Authentic Athletic Performance.

Taco Bell's goal was to embody the soul of the brand in the food, to remind consumers that Taco Bell is different from burgers and fries. The core concept—"Not the same old fare"—was expressed to consumers as "Think Outside the Bun."

Know Your Customer

Where does your customer shop? How? When? What does he or she read or watch? Those channels and media are where your customer and brand touch. And where your integration effort must focus.

Marketers at Circuit City had identified their best customer segment as young males. Using new analytic tools, they discovered their best customers were middle-aged dads—crazy about electronics, but lacking knowledge of all the gadgets and insecure about making product choices. This strategic insight was captured in a new line: "We know how you feel. And that's why we're here. WE'RE WITH YOU."

With this core idea, advertising spending was shifted from mainly promotional inserts in newspapers to a multimedia campaign that included event marketing and public relations—all the ways this information-hungry customer researches the category.

Look for Big Ideas with "Legs"

Integrated campaigns are built on big ideas that translate well into many media and many channels. However, small elements are important because they tie things together. Graphics, design, and tone of voice should be distinctive and consistent at every level.

Apple has always been scrupulous in following its brand guidelines to communicate simplicity and ease of use. Whether a print ad, direct mail piece, or web site, their designers' use of white space and simple product shots is distinctively Apple.

It helps to have a style guide to the brand including brand strategy and mantra, plus guides for graphics, photography and illustration, sound and animation, and examples for all media and channels—for advertiser and agency. Since several organizations will probably be involved, the guide should be produced jointly by the creative leaders from each discipline and approved by the advertiser.

It takes great collaborators to make integration work. "Not invented here" is hard to subdue, and it is often difficult to work with people whose discipline you don't know much about. Bringing team members together helps smooth the way. Whether in large meetings or smaller working sessions, there is no substitute for building personal relationships. All team members must understand and support the campaign enthusiastically, then aim to create world-class work in their area.

Many organizations establish strong graphic guidelines ("templates") because they simplify the integration process. Unfortunately, rigid templates make every communication look the same. In a year-long series with hundreds of targeted communications, that can be disastrous.

Be strict about the core idea and the general look and feel of the brand, within reasonable guidelines. Rely on the lead art director or designer to make important decisions on logo and graphics. Don't let "logo cops"—people without design or art direction experience—make these calls.

Integration Takes Commitment

It takes time and money to build an integrated campaign that is effective in every channel. While the advertising may launch in January, it could take a full year for all customer communications to be reprogrammed and designed.

The advertising may be refreshed from time to time, but it must stay true to the core brand elements—strategy, graphics, voice. Even a seemingly small thing like changing the typeface can wreak havoc across all the integrating groups.

Integrated communications requires a mandate from the advertiser's top management. Without that, most business unit heads or product managers will be loath to change creative that is working. Or they will simply want to do things their own way.

The obstacles are on both sides of the fence—agency and advertiser. Some agencies are learning to integrate their organizations to deliver total communications solutions, but it takes dedication and special training to overcome internal cost structures and turf defenses.

When the advertiser has a full-service agency partner, it alleviates much of the problem. Otherwise, it can become a full-time job to pull together several different firms whose only common ground is working for the same client.

The potential benefits are large. The need for commitment is enormous. But nobody said it would be easy.

PART II

Getting the Message Out

8 Television

It's getting harder all the time to get viewers to pay attention to your commercial. Most advertising messages are ignored. Clutter is real—the average person is exposed to over 2,500 advertising messages a day in all kinds of media. Research has shown that most viewers can't remember a typical commercial one day after they've seen it. Now new technology like the Personal Video Recorder joins the remote control in helping consumers skip over commercials. Is *anybody* watching?

"What drives this business is the never ending search for some new way to wake up the audience," says one industry pro.

TV viewing patterns are also changing. Broadcast TV remains the great mass medium by a wide margin. Although the major networks have been losing audience share to other TV options for several decades, people are watching more TV than ever (four hours a day on average). It is everywhere—in office elevators (and offices), in dentists' offices, in airports (and on planes), on stadium scoreboards . . . around the world.

Still, individual TV options are less mass than before. Audience ratings on individual shows are down to half of what they were not long ago. Cable TV now reaches about 75 percent of homes, and some U.S. homes can receive 500 channels—new opportunities for targeted programming, niche marketing, foreign-language stations, community news, telemarketing channels (some call them "flea TV"), current movies at any hour.

Other than causing some expected loss among younger viewers, the internet has not had much of an impact on total TV viewing. However, the number of people watching TV and surfing the web *simultaneously* continues to rise—Gartner Inc. calls them "telewebbers." As more people get broadband connections in their homes, interactivity (in viewing and shopping) is likely to increase.

While none of these devices has materially dented television, network levels are down, and more people switch to another channel when commercials come on (says Roper Research). The challenge is to create advertising that people *want* to watch—or follow them where they go (to other media).

THE KEY IS INVOLVEMENT

How can you get people to watch your advertising?

Not with a commercial that shouts. The best way to get your audience to watch your commercial is to involve them, so they *want* to watch. You must grab viewers with a meaningful promise wrapped in a strong creative idea.

There are several routes.

Create a situation with which they identify.

A middle-aged couple with two teenagers discusses the slightly embarrassing fact that she is pregnant. The husband says: "So when he starts college . . ." and the wife completes his sentence, "We'll be 60." He laughs, because the situation is both crazy and welcome.

Present a problem to which you have the solution.

There's one almost sure-fire way to make your commercial memorable and attention-getting—start by presenting a problem viewers will understand and for which your product or service is the solution.

"The shipping department is out sick. What are we going to do?" Solution—FedEx.

Provide information they want.

"I didn't know." "I didn't know." "I didn't know." A chorus of voices confesses ignorance that recurring heartburn could be something serious. This spot introduces "a purple pill called Nexium" for heartburn relief, and suggests that viewers call an 800 number for more facts.

Give them appropriate entertainment.

Tiger Woods bounces a golf ball on the face of a club 15 or 20 times. Then he flips it up in the air and hits a perfect shot. It's pure entertainment—and compelling television for Nike.

Great advertising provides some reward for watching. It is relevant to people's needs, interests, values, or lifestyles.

HOW TO READ A STORYBOARD

A commercial is usually presented in the form of a "storyboard" that pictures the main action of the spot and describes what the viewer will see (the video) and hear (the audio). It may include some technical terms such as VO (voice-over) or CU (close-up).

The *wrong* way to read a storyboard is to get overly involved in the "audio" of the spot. The visuals do the heavy lifting. People remember and react to what they see—that's why they're called viewers. Try covering up the words and asking yourself what is the message of the commercial with the sound turned off. Is there a message at all?

How can you look at these tiny illustrations and few words and know whether or not they will translate into a persuasive, memorable piece of advertising? Casting and special effects are particularly hard to visualize. It helps to look at clips from movies or television to understand the kind of actors wanted or to demonstrate unusual production techniques.

The larger issue is what you should look for in a storyboard.

Is the key consumer benefit the central and most compelling idea of the commercial?

If it isn't, *turn it down.* You'll never have an easier decision. It may be the funniest storyboard you've every seen, or the most heartrending, but if it doesn't focus on the relevant selling idea, you will be spending a lot of time and money on a commercial that will fail.

The agency may disagree and point out exactly where in the storyboard the benefit is being delivered. So it may be your judgment against theirs. But a good advertising agency should never show you creative work that is off-strategy.

Here are some other pitfalls to watch for.

- Does your brand and core benefit appear only in the last few seconds of the spot?
- Is the benefit mouthed by a voice-over announcer while visuals show something else?
- Does the "plot" of the commercial pivot around your brand and its benefit, or could a different advertiser be substituted?
- If the spot depends on humor, is the fun overwhelming the strategy?

Once you have determined that a storyboard is indeed communicating the strategy, decide whether it will make an *effective* television spot. Here are some guidelines.

MORE EFFECTIVE TELEVISION COMMERCIALS

1. The pictures should tell the story. Television is a visual medium, and some of the most riveting and memorable spots require few words—or none at all.

> *Lightning flashes over New York City and all the lights blink off. In this total darkness, the Statue of Liberty consults her watch, which lights up to show the time. Only ten words of copy are used. "Timex Indiglo Night Light. No woman should be without one."*

Here's another test you can apply to a storyboard. Can you pick out a *key visual*—one frame that visually sums up the whole idea?

Watch out for "just as, so too" executions, such as showing a concert pianist to represent a financial services firm ("To reach the top takes years of work and practice").

2. Grab the viewer's attention. The first 5 to 10 seconds of a commercial are crucial—they will either hold the audience or lose it. Analysis of audience attention shows that interest holds steady or drops sharply as the commercial opens—it does not rise. Viewers must find something immediately they want to watch.

> *It's hard not to watch a spot for Orkin exterminators as a cockroach appears to crawl on the surface of the TV screen.*

Go for surprise openings, not surprise endings. And don't insult your viewers' intelligence by trying to gain their interest with a gimmick that has nothing to do with the brand strategy.

3. Be single-minded. A good commercial is sharply focused on *one idea*—the key consumer benefit. It's hard enough to communicate one idea and the reason to believe it. Trying to deliver more is almost impossible.

A corollary is simplicity. Don't ask viewers to work at trying to figure out your message. They won't.

Dunkin' Donuts used its long-time spokesman, the counterman, to announce a new offering—iced coffee. The commercial simply showed him ice-skating for the entire 30 seconds, executing leaps and spins, while holding a pot of coffee.

In another commercial, the counterman is pursued by a giant rolling bagel, to announce this addition to the menu.

Simple storyboards can fool you. They may look dull on paper, but TV is a medium that thrives on simplicity. Conversely, a fascinating storyboard often translates into a busy commercial that is hard to follow. A good commercial is simple, clear, and uncomplicated.

Longer commercials should not add copy points. The basic commercial length in the U.S. remains 30 seconds. Longer commercials, whether :45s or :60s, tell the same story with more time for mood and emotion. It is interesting how much can be packed into shorter commercials—:15s or even :10s.

When your campaign includes several message lengths, look at the shortest first. If the message cannot be delivered effectively in that time, you're not being single-minded.

4. Pre-empt the idea for your brand. A vintage book called *Obvious Adams* told of a young copywriter who could look at the obvious and find revelations. Assigned to a beer account, he marveled that the brewery washed its bottles in live steam. "Every brewery does that," he was told. "Ah," he said, "but no other brewery is talking about it."

Dawn dishwashing liquid was launched with the promise that it encapsulates grease and keeps it away from your hands. It was a powerful positioning. Few consumers realized that's exactly how all dishwashing liquids work.

It's hard to have a unique product these days, since the competition can copy your technology so rapidly. But if you can own an *idea*, you effectively shut out your competitors, unless they want to look like copycats.

5. Make sure the spot has "stickyness." Will your target audience remember your commercial and your brand next week or even next month? Memorability is especially important if your product isn't an everyday purchase like soap or toothpaste.

Here are a few tried-and-true ways to make sure your advertising "sticks."

Show people, not objects.
Your commercial will be better remembered and probably more persuasive if you show people rather than inanimate objects.

On a rainy night, a young man holding an umbrella over his head rings a doorbell. A young woman opens the door. He is so mesmerized by her appearance that he lowers the umbrella and simply stands there in the pouring rain, gazing at her. "Reinvent the compliment" is the tagline for this no-words-needed spot for Nordstrom.

 Remember that people speaking on camera command higher recall for the message than a disembodied announcer voice-over.

Have a payoff.

At some point, show that your product does what you say it will do. The young couple should drink the soft drink, the dog should eat the dog food.

> *A bachelor lives alone except for a number of pets, including a dog, a cockatoo, and a ram. He cooks a hot dog, wolfs it down, and begins to choke. The dog sits up, the bird flutters, and the ram charges over to butt him in the stomach, performing a Heimlich Maneuver. A perfect payoff for Animal Planet's positioning line—"Life is better with animals."*

Register the brand name.

Sometimes a viewer will remember the commercial but not the name of the product or service, particularly if it is new or unfamiliar. It takes more than repetition to make a name stick.

- *New pharmaceutical products face a particular challenge, because the name of the brand often has no meaning to the consumer.*
  Relenza, a flu remedy, helped people remember with a little rhyme. "If your doctor says it's influenza, ask about Relenza."
- *People are discussing insurance, a duck enters the scene and quacks "AFLAC!" They don't get it, and the duck, increasingly annoyed, quacks the brand name over and over.*

Brand names that start with "soft" consonants—*m*'s and *n*'s for example—are more difficult to keep in mind than those with "hard" ones like *t*'s or *k*'s. That's why George Eastman invented the name Kodak for his cameras, and why names like Coke and Tide are so easy to remember.

6. Reflect your brand personality. It takes dedication and consistency to maintain a brand personality. You may see storyboards that tempt you to take it in a different direction. Remember that a brand personality is hard-won and easily destroyed, so discipline yourself to reject any advertising that conflicts with it.

> *The commercial opens with the theme from* Easy Rider, *showing a young Peter Fonda on a chopped motorcycle next to a middle-aged man (also riding one), white shirt and tie flying in the wind.*
>
> *Cut to commuter bus with the middle-aged guy (now with music headset) screeching the* Easy Rider *theme while his fellow passengers—eyebrows raised, peek out from behind their papers.*
>
> *A Pepsi commercial, it works for Gen Y and X (they get to laugh at the old guy) and takes the brand into the Baby Boomer world (they get to be the center of attention and relive their youth).*

It often helps to have a written personality statement of your product. If it were a person, what sort of individual would it be?

Chevrolet was built with advertising that started with a description of a guy named Joe.

> *Joe is 27 years old. He's a former Marine. He's not a genius, but he is a smart guy. Gregarious, a man of the people, likes girls, a family man. Works hard at his job, but* loves sports.

7. **Less is more.** When you ask for ten words to be added to a commercial, identify which ten you'd delete to make room for them.

Don't try to jam everything into your commercial. You'll bury your message.

WHICH DRAMATIC FORM WORKS BEST FOR YOU?

There are many dramatic paths, and they are timeless—some go as far back as the Bible. The parable tells a little story, just like a slice of life. The parting of the Red Sea is a demonstration. Job's statement of faith is a testimonial. Moses, with the Ten Commandments, is the ultimate spokesperson. The Bible is full of tried-and-true appeals, like emotion and sex.

TV advertising uses a number of these dramatic techniques. Each has a particular strength, and one may be more appropriate than another for your brand. They are not mutually exclusive—a demonstration is frequently used in a testimonial or a slice-of-life.

Demonstrations—the most powerful technique of all

If you can show people what your product does, or the fact that it does something better than the competition, *show it*. Seeing is believing.

> *Kodak dramatizes the digital features of its MC3 camera with a young man filming snippets of images to spell an e-mailed invitation to his girl—Sushi tonight? ("raw" from a store name, fish [picture], "2," "knight" from a sign).*

A demonstration, if done well, will always be the most memorable element in your commercial, so make sure it is proving the key consumer benefit of your strategy.

Testimonials—to make a point believable

When you can't demonstrate a product advantage, consumers have to take your word for it. It may be more persuasive to offer the words of fellow consumers who testify that in their experience, the product does what you claim. Bear in mind that your testimonees must stick with the facts. If someone says your detergent gets clothes whiter, you need research that proves it.

Testimonials say to the viewer: "This is the truth." There is an authenticity about real people that is hard for actors to simulate—an awkward pause, garbled syntax, some disarming clumsiness.

To avoid testimonials that are simply "talking heads," it helps to have an executional idea that goes beyond the technique.

- *The hidden camera, where the testimonees discover they are being filmed.*
- *The "restaged" testimonial, where the person repeats for the camera statements he or she has made previously to an interviewer, not knowing a commercial was involved.*
- *The testimonial with a twist, where a loyal user is offered money to switch to a competitive product.*

People delivering the testimonials may be ordinary men and women. They may be celebrities or noncelebrity experts (a racing car driver for a motor oil). An average consumer with an above-average involvement in the category can also become an expert, like mothers talking about the best diapers for infants.

Spokespersons—to symbolize the brand

Whether they are actors, celebrities, executives, or created personalities, the best spokespeople are those who go beyond the message and build a strong image for the brand. There are exceptions, but few CEOs have the TV presence that the spokesperson role demands.

Do celebrities attract attention to themselves and get in the way of the message? Actually, the contrary is true. Research suggests that the *appropriate* celebrity will increase both attention value and persuasion.

> *Pepsi could not have chosen a more appropriate celebrity than Britney Spears to epitomize the brand's "Think Young" positioning.*

Be aware that celebrities present risks. They can get sick, or just get into trouble.

Slice-of-life—to involve people with the brand

It's the oldest dramatic technique of all—actors telling a story. A little play unfolds, inviting people to become involved with the brand, which holds center stage. Often it opens with a problem to which the brand is the solution.

The slice is a powerful technique that doesn't have to be corny at all. The use of realistic situations, honest dialogue, emotion, or humor can make this technique soar.

> *The 37-year-old son, living at home with his family, insists that he is still a kid. "And kids should stay for free and eat for free," he protests. "What do you think this is," his father asks, "a Holiday Inn?"*

"Mikey," a memorable slice for Life cereal about the hard-to-feed four-year-old, is the kind of timeless spot that connects with people across generations. It first ran in 1972 and was revived with great success 28 years later.

Animation—primarily to reach children

Think of Tony the Tiger growling for Kellogg's Frosted Flakes.

Watch Saturday morning television and you'll quickly see the appeal of cartoon animation for cereals, candy, toys, or any other product principally directed at children. Cartoon techniques range from full animation to characters "roto-scoped" in combination with the reality of film. New technology constantly reduces costs and time to produce animation, and offers up new ideas for creative teams to try.

Cartoons can also talk to adults. Among the classics is the Pink Panther for pink Owens-Corning Fiberglas.

Competitive advertising—to challenge the competition

Naming names—like "the Pepsi Challenge," in which Coca-Cola was shown to lose in taste tests—continues to be a popular way to challenge established market leaders. This is not the same as comparative advertising, in which the "other leading brand" is never named.

Identifying competition is a high-risk technique. Research shows that viewers are often confused as to which brand is being advertised or why one brand is better than another. Amid all the controversy, there seems to be one point of agreement—don't advertise your competitor if you are the market leader.

Sex—in its place

The effectiveness of sex as an advertising technique depends largely on its relevance. The days when advertisers tried to sell cars by draping shapely girls over the hood are fading. Sex works best when it grows out of the consumer benefit—that's why it is so often used in cosmetics and fragrance advertising.

Two classic sexy commercials came from outside those categories.

- *A woman's voice, accompanied by strip-tease music, urges a man to "Take it off. Take it all off." (Noxzema shaving cream)*

- *A beautiful young Brooke Shields confesses, "Nothing comes between me and my Calvins." (Calvin Klein Jeans)*

Humor—the most popular technique of all

Frogs croaking "Bud-weis-er" were a long-running and successful use of humor in this campaign, which added lizards to the cast.

Think about the most popular Super Bowl commercials of the past ten years. Seven out of ten of them involved humor. The One Club, a creative group, decided to name the "best commercials of the past century." Of the winning 30, more than two-thirds were humorous. Without question, humor, when it is truly funny, entertains. The question remains—does it sell?

Is the humor overpowering the message? If you can remove your product, but the joke remains intact, chances are that it has nothing to do with the key benefit.

Jerry Seinfeld's humor is integral to the message in spots demonstrating how the American Express Card can be used in supermarkets, mass merchandisers, and other retail establishments.

Keep several cautions in mind when you look at a "funny" storyboard. First, humor is a very difficult technique. That's why the late-night talk shows have so many writers who get paid so much money. If you agree the spot is truly funny, ask yourself how it will play to your target audience.

One last caution—humor wears out fast, so you will need more spots to keep your campaign fresh.

Music—to cue the viewer's feelings

Music is powerful emotional shorthand. It can tell the viewer how to feel by evoking feelings—of joy, of serenity, of love, of fear.

> *A demonstration film to make this point showed a young woman swimming in a moonlit sea. With background music of Debussy's* La Mer, *it was romantic. The same film, with the music from* Jaws, *evoked fear.*

Music can be written especially for the advertising. You will have to pay somebody to write the music and lyrics. If you want musicians and singers to record it, you'll have to pay each one a fee for the session, plus residuals when the spot runs. If you decide to use a full-size symphony orchestra, it gets even more expensive.

Or you can license a song from the vast existing repertory from popular to classic. That's the route Mercedes-Benz took when it used the old Marlene Dietrich song "Falling in Love Again" to show different generations of people delighting in the car.

Using a familiar song can be effective if it enhances the core idea, but it is almost always expensive. Copyrights run as long as 85 years, so much popular music is not in the public domain. Costs can run into the millions of dollars, depending on how hot the artist is and broadly you plan to use the spot.

Beware of using existing music when you are testing commercials in an "animatic" (still pictures on film). Testing a well-known song performed by a famous singer may boost your score, but prove to be unattainable or beyond your budget.

The least expensive solution is usually stock music, but it's affordable because it's not exclusive. You might find that the distinctive music you have selected for your coffee commercial is also being used for a hemorrhoid medication.

Often the best music is music you don't know is there. A rough cut of a commercial, not yet scored, may seem flat and lacking drama. The musical punctuation—emphasizing a car's swerve on the road, for example—tells the viewer how to feel.

Then there are nonmusical sound effects like doors slamming or crickets chirping. Combined with music, this is called "sound design." In the hands of a skilled designer, it can add dimension—drama, humor, emotion—to your spot.

HOW TO CONTROL COMMERCIAL PRODUCTION COSTS

Television commercials have become incredibly expensive. An average 30-second spot costs between $350,000 and $500,000 to produce—"extravaganzas" twice that much.

Before creative work begins, tell the agency what your production budget is. If it is limited, challenge the creative team to come up with a memorable idea that can be produced for the money available.

> *A new water park asked its agency to do something involving but relatively inexpensive. Instead of the usual large cast of happy swimmers, the agency filmed one little boy on his backyard slide on a hot August day. Heat waves shimmer, cicadas chirp, and you hear the "chalk against blackboard" sound of the kid's sticky body moving down the slide. "It's going to be a long, hot summer," the announcer says, inviting viewers to visit the park.*

Production should not exceed 10 percent of your media budget—you want advertising dollars going into "working" media to the greatest extent possible. However, a smaller brand in a big-image category may spend considerably more, as much as a third of the media budget.

One way to control costs is to steer away from items that almost always mean additional costs—a celebrity spokesperson, elaborate sets, multiple locations, special film techniques. Are you looking at a strong concept or one that relies too heavily on technique and production values?

Television production is a process that encompasses three phases—pre-production (agreeing on specifications for the storyboard, getting bids, awarding the job, hammering out the details), production, and post-production.

Allow enough time. Television production expert Patrick Collins says a simple live-action 30-second spot with no special effects needs a minimum of nine weeks from approval of the storyboard to completion of the final master. He adds that you can do it more quickly, but will risk additional costs. The rule of thumb—four weeks for pre-production (bids from production companies, casting, wardrobe, set design or location scouting), one week for production, four weeks for post-production (rough cuts, approvals, the almost inevitable revisions, online finish, titles and visual effects, music, sound effects scoring, titles, and final master).

Pre-production

Get the necessary approvals, including those from your own and the agency's legal departments, and Continuity Clearance from any networks where you plan to run the spot. You and the agency need to develop your detailed "wish list" for the commercial, known as "specifications," which will guide the production company in figuring out costs. The usual next step is to get bids from at least three production houses as a frame of reference. You don't need to select the lowest bid—you simply want the best creative thinking for the dollars available.

Most production companies work with a roster of directors. Ask your agency to show you reels of the best directors for this particular commercial. For example, you may want someone especially adept at comedy, or fast action, or appetite appeal. For a great idea, some directors (and especially young ones starting out) may agree to work for a minimum to get the spot on their reel.

Once the production company is selected, it will do a "shooting board," which presents a scene-by-scene and shot-by-shot roadmap of what will be filmed. Everyone involved attends the Pre-Production Meeting, held at least two days before the filming begins. You, or someone from your company, with the power to approve or disapprove, should be there.

Production

There is one immutable law of production—*always shoot the agreed-upon storyboard.*

The director may come up with new ideas and add additional scenes. That's fine, as long as they don't take you into overtime. Insist, first of all, that the original board be filmed or taped as approved.

Another helpful hint from the old hands—*if anything looks wrong or sounds wrong or feels wrong, speak up.*

Protocol for clients at a shoot is to give your comments to the advertising agency producer, not to the director or actors. Finally, there must be someone on the set who can make on-the-spot decisions. Suppose the demonstration doesn't work, the actor can't say the words, or the script needs to be cut for time. Revisions must be filmed right there—reshoots are prohibitively expensive.

Post-production

Thanks to digital technology, editing has become a fast and precise process. The director or the editor (or both) can look at different versions and decide whether one-half second more or less better drives home humor or sets up the key benefit.

The agency usually shows you one or two of these "rough cuts," which are without sound effects, special effects, color correction, or music. Once you have approved the cuts or seen them with revisions you requested, this "locked picture" goes to online finish including a finished soundtrack, titles (such as your tagline) and effects (such as "dissolves").

With a strong concept, you may be able to achieve the ultimate cost saving—the need to make fewer commercials. Nobody yet has come with a foolproof formula to measure "wear out." Generally, we take commercials off the air long before consumers are tired of them. Too much money is wasted on producing unnecessary commercials. Spend your advertising dollars on the TV screen, not in the studio.

Does it Have Legs?

Successful brands are built on communicating the same thing, over and over, with variations on a theme. So when you look at new advertising, ask yourself if this is an ad or a campaign. How far can it stretch?

One way to decide if a storyboard is a potential campaign is to pretend you are going to write the next commercial. Ideas must be able to extend into other media, and go on in time.

When you look at a storyboard, ask yourself:

- Does it contain an idea?
- Is the idea relevant to the selling message?
- Will the advertising reward the viewer for paying attention?
- Will it work in other media? Can it run for years? *Does it have legs?*

9 Magazines and Newspapers

Forget everything in this chapter but this one guideline, and you'll be ahead of the game.

Put your message in the headline or visual of every print advertisement, ideally in both.

Most readers never reach the text or body copy. If the message is not in the headline or visual, the reader simply won't get it. Many effective print ads now work like posters, where the picture tells the story and few (if any) words are needed.

The illustration—a bottle of Absolut Mandarin vodka perched on an orange squeezer. The headline—"Absolut Squeeze."

The illustration—a huge lemon. The headline—"Absolut Citron."

There are categories—travel, technology, money, and health—where readers are hungry for information. For these, long copy (even multipage ads) work.

IBM introduced its "e-business on demand" service with an eight-page long-copy newspaper insert.

These are exceptions. For the most part, it's the headline and illustration that do the work.

Consumers are spending more time than ever with all forms of media, but tend to use them simultaneously. In a recent survey, 73 percent of the respondents admitted to having read a magazine while watching television!

Don't let the copywriter read you the copy—print advertising doesn't work that way. When you look at a rough ad, try to react to the overall impression. Does it have stopping power? Think of your reader as wielding a remote control that turns the pages.

Scan the ads in any magazine and notice how few offer a strong, clear benefit, either in headline or visual. Look at the articles in the same magazines, with titles like these.

"Lose 10 pounds this month"

"Find the 25th hour"

"Groove your swing"

"Unclutter your closet"

"How to raise happy, self-confident, well-liked kids"

Magazine editor John Mack Carter believes the secret of print is *emotionally involving the reader*. His editors listen carefully to the audience and respond with articles that speak to their interests. A good clue for advertisers seeking emotional involvement.

The illustration, the face of a little girl, is filled with meaning from the headline: "Cancer. Where you're treated first can make all the difference."

The copy makes the case for Memorial Sloan-Kettering Cancer Center, and finishes: "So if someone you love is diagnosed with cancer, call us first for the help—and hope—you need.

Research firm Mapes & Ross suggests that persuasion and recall will be stronger if the advertisement immediately lets the reader know what category your product or service fits in. If the ad suggests you are selling cake mixes when you are actually in financial services, readers feel vaguely cheated—robbed of the "reward" they deserve for giving the advertisement their time and attention.

MasterCard makes clear it is selling financial services:

"financial advice for your son: $6 phone call"

"home buying advice for your son: $9 phone call"

"child rearing advice for your son: $15"

Then the emotional benefit—"your son realizing you do know what you're talking about: priceless."

Magazines—For Special Interests

Despite dire predictions that the internet would kill off magazines and newspapers, Americans continue to read. There are still thousands of consumer magazines published in the U.S., although publishers have grown more cautious about launching new titles. The success story of the past decade is, of course, O, *the Oprah Winfrey Magazine*. Its success is founded in part on Oprah and in part on the magazine's content.

> *"Women admire her in every way. They adore her and aspire to be like her. They also want the information, the service, and the substance—the ideas in food, beauty, and fashion."*
>
> —CATHIE BLACK, PRESIDENT, HEARST MAGAZINES

Mass magazines have declined slightly, while special-interest titles—magazines about teenagers, men's health, technology, and gardening—continue to grow. Some magazines, such as *National Geographic* and *Better Homes & Gardens*, have spawned television networks. And networks have given birth to magazines, including *ESPN The Magazine*, A&E's *Biography*, and *This Old House*.

Magazines can be even more selective with special editions. *BusinessWeek* offers five demographic or special editions:

- *Elite*—targeting the most affluent. Delivered to subscribers who receive *BW* at home and live in high-income zip codes.
- *Elite Bonus*—*BW* and *Golf Digest* joint editorial features to reach affluent readers of both publications.
- *Industrial Management*—U.S. and Canadian subscribers employed as executives in the industrial and manufacturing sectors.
- *BusinessWeek Small Biz*—Owners, managers, and professionals in companies with fewer than 100 employees.
- *BusinessWeek e.biz*—Business and technology professionals.

The great opportunity print often provides is the ability to reach an audience that has a special interest in the publication and is likely to be paying close attention. Readers expect information in print—they accept and even seek out ads as part of the medium, as retailers and publishers of fashion magazines know.

But they can also easily turn the page.

Newspapers—A News Environment

The big news in newspapers is *national* newspapers—*USA Today, The New York Times*, and *The Wall Street Journal*, which reach affluent and educated consumers across the country. Daily local papers, once the dominant medium, are falling behind as 24-hour cable networks and internet news sites cut into traditional news coverage (and profitable classified advertising). Weeklies are up, as are "alternative titles" (free weekly papers with special emphasis on entertainment) and free shoppers' papers.

"The beauty of newspapers is they make things feel newsworthy," says Bob Austin, director of marketing communications for Volvo, which used newspapers to help relaunch its luxury S80 sedan.

Newspapers are a great announcement medium.

> *"Introducing ONE Less Concern in Your Life" was the headline that launched the American Express ONE Financial Account.*

"Newspaper is a special medium," writes Creative Director Lee Clow. "It's URGENT. Not yesterday or tomorrow but TODAY, so the message has to demand ATTENTION."

WHAT WORKS BEST IN PRINT

The first principle:

> **React to the overall impression of the entire advertisement.**

Does it clearly deliver the core benefit of the strategy? The benefit must be quickly and easily apparent—the reader will not spend time puzzling over the ad. If the concept needs words to convey the idea, put them in the headline.

- *A photo of a very young Chinese girl figure skating. The headline—"Career path: State, Nationals, Olympics, Pros, Retirement, High School. You may not get it, but our 24 million readers do.* Sports Illustrated.*"*

- *A full-page ad during the baseball season shows Texas Rangers star Rafael Palmiero, with his impressive statistics, followed by the headline, "I take Viagra. Let's just say it works for me."*
- *The illustration—a photo of the handicapped parking symbol. The headline—"At many companies, some of the hardest workers have the best parking spaces." The ad for the National Organization on Disability makes the case for hiring people with disabilities.*
- *A photo of a BMW on the road catches your eye with the headline, "You save $960,530." Then you notice above it, "Cost $39,470. Feels like $1,000,000."*

It's simply not enough to put the benefit in the body copy, because most people today, especially those under thirty, don't bother to read it. In fact, evidence from focus groups suggests that long copy is so off-putting to young readers, they will skip over the ad altogether. And don't let a copywriter tell you that a "blind" headline, one that contains no message about the brand ("Amazing Offer," "Home run"), will entice the reader into the body copy. It won't.

Here are some other fundamental principles for effective print advertising.

1. Reward your readers. Give them something for their time and attention—news, service (a recipe), appetite appeal, or emotional gratification.

Hallmark Cards wanted to convey that a card can have a big impact on people's lives for very little money. One ad in the campaign showed a husband and wife sharing a tender moment over a card. The headline: "Marriage counseling. 99 cents."

 Information is a reward.

To attract executive readers, Sun Microsystems offers readers perspectives under the headline "Long-Term Strategies in a Short-Term World"—covering topics such as "Yellow-Light Leadership" and "When and Why Do CEOs Leave?"

2. **Look for story appeal in the visual.** Find something that makes the reader say: "That looks interesting. I think I'll find out more about it."

- *Volkswagen decided to refresh its "New Beetle" advertising, but wanted to continue to emphasize the car's striking design. The new campaign revolved around the idea that the shape and color of a Volkswagen is so noticeable, it attracts attention even in extraordinary situations. One ad shows people at the running of the bulls in Pamplona. They have stopped in their tracks to look at the car, calling out "Hey, there's a yellow one."*
- *A young woman beseechingly hands a pot of flowers to a soldier with gas mask and club. A red outline of the cover of* Time *magazine surrounds the flowers.*
- *A series of striking photographs of American Express celebrity Cardmembers was given story appeal by photographer Annie Leibovitz—barefoot 7' basketball star Wilt Chamberlain standing next to 5' jockey Willie Shoemaker, tuxedo-clad Sammy Davis, Jr., dancing in the [Las Vegas] desert, barefoot House Speaker Tip O'Neill in a beach chair under a beach umbrella.*

There is nothing inherently interesting in product-as-hero visuals—unless they are done with a difference (like

Absolut's bottle-as-hero ads). Research suggests that some of the most effective visuals tell the whole story of the advertisement without a word of copy needed.

An ad for Evian simply showed a goldfish swimming happily in a bowl being filled with the product. No headline was needed.

The visual is almost always more important than the headline.

3. Use demonstrations. One of the most successful editorial formats in women's magazines is the "makeover"—dramatic demonstrations of the transformation after weight loss, makeup, and hair restyling or a new wardrobe. The same formula applies to home design and other categories.

Demonstrations work in TV—why not print?

To support its promise that its printer makes copies "true to the original," Hewlett-Packard uses a photograph of a field of flowers from which a square (the copy) has been carved out and displayed separately. The two visuals match perfectly.

4. Photography increases readership. Research shows that photography increases recall an average of 26 percent over artwork. It is always preferable to artwork when showing food. Showing the completed dish has more appetite appeal than showing raw ingredients.

Can you put a caption under the photo? Picture captions get twice as much readership as body copy. Travel magazines know this—notice how often they rely on photo captions to draw the reader into the article.

5. Color increases readership. A Roper Starch Worldwide survey reported that full-color newspaper ads were "Read Most" 61 percent more often than black-and-white ads.

 The same survey also debunked some myths—right-hand pages are no more effective than left-hand ones and, contrary to concerns about clutter, pages with as many as nine ads garnered the same attention as pages with only three.

6. Build strong, distinctive campaigns. Does your advertising have a format that sets it apart from the rest? Put your ad on the wall, together with a group of competitive ads. Step back and ask yourself if your ad stands out. Recognition of your brand can be doubled with the right campaign.

- *Smiling celebrities sporting a "milk moustache" created a recognizable campaign for milk.*
- *Nike introduced its new all-weather Air Pegasus running shoe with a three-page advertisement. The first page was a large photo of a muddy, wet, and well-worn Nike shoe. The following two-page spread juxtaposed a rainy but inviting trail with the monotonous diagrams found on running machines. The only words needed—"Enjoy the weather."*

7. Make each ad a complete sale. Don't assume the reader will read every advertisement in a campaign. Each ad must be a complete sale. The basic proposition should be presented in its entirety every time—including reasons to believe the benefit.

The best campaigns, like the best strategies, are tightly held variations on a theme.

To make the point that technology can deliver a true consumer benefit, a Motorola ad shows a milk carton with the headline: "I'm spoiled." A refrigerator on the facing page says, "I know."

In another spread, a sweater says, "Be gentle." A washing machine responds, "I will."

8. Integrate online and offline solutions. Newspapers have been among the most aggressive media players in offering clients both a web and a print solution.

> The New York Times *offered New Line Cinema a print and web solution for the launch of its film* Lord of the Rings. *Full-page ads announced the opening and pointed to a special web-only feature on NYTimes.com, where readers could browse through a complete guide to J.R.R. Tolkien, including the original 1954 book review of* The Hobbitt.

9. Break out of the mold. Print can do things that television cannot. It can deliver a coupon, allow room for information, provide services such as recipes, and, in some ambitious examples, do it all at the same time while building a strong brand image, as well.

> *Grey Goose Vodka created a special eight-page advertisement for* The New Yorker*—a combination of sophisticated cartoons in the magazine's style and several pages of product sell (how to make a Cosmopolitan cocktail) plus results of taste tests.*
>
> *One cartoon with the headline "All in Good Taste" showed two young women at a bar. One says of a single man at a nearby table, "He just ordered a Grey Goose Vodka. At least I'll respect him in the morning."*

During holiday seasons, magazines trail clouds of fragrance from scratch-and-sniff advertisements, while microchips embedded in their pages deliver carols. The growth of special print units, as these are known, includes attention-getters like a motion-sickness bag attached to a Mini car ad, to illustrate adventurous driving. As one publisher put it, "We have a limitation to how many advertisers we can put forward in the magazine."

10. Design the advertisement for the medium. Size makes a difference. Don't take an advertisement designed for a large-format magazine and just reduce it for *Reader's Digest*. It must be redesigned specifically for the smaller magazine, using cropped photos to suggest what appears in the larger units.

Take editorial content into consideration. Some advertisers have discovered that it pays to run ads that are "themed" for sports or music or high-tech magazines, or to take a different approach in a fashion magazine than in a newsmagazine. They say the increased attention and readership make up for the additional production costs.

There's a vast difference, too, between paper stocks. The subtle colors that can be reproduced on expensive coated stock are one thing—what will reproduce well on uncoated newspaper stock is another. You must plan for publications that offer less definition or less sharp color.

Look at the advertisement in context, not just mounted for presentation. Ask that it be pasted up in the publication.

Techniques That Reduce Readership.

Be on your guard if the art director tries to sell you one of these.

"Addy" layouts. Research says that readers are turned away by layouts that look cluttered, have lots of little pictures or a jumble of typefaces. Help the reader through your ad with subheads, a strong lead-in paragraph (or at least lead sentence), preferably set in bold type, and devices such as numbers or bullets instead of long, run-on sentences.

"Wall-to-wall" copy. A solid block of copy looks like too much work to today's prose-phobic readers. They

will turn the page. Invite the reader in with paragraph breaks and copy set in columns, separated by lots of white space.

Setting copy in reverse, such as white copy against a dark or multicolored background. It makes a visual statement, but says that we don't really care if you read this.

Headlines with words in several different sizes. Art directors have seized on this trend—they love to set unimportant words like "the" in large typeface and relegate your benefit to a lesser size.

"Eccentric" fonts, such as Olde English. Avoid these unless you are selling English manors.

Sans-serif typeface (which looks like this*) for body copy.* Use a serif typeface, in which this book is set.

Using a logo in place of the brand name in headline or copy. People don't "read" logos.

"Mice type" (8-point or smaller). Most of the copy in this book is set in 11.5-point type.

"Make sure every ad coming out of your agency is readable," urges agency head Jerry Della Femina. Instead of using 8-point type, use 10; instead of 10-point, make it 12. Producing a pro bono campaign for Lighthouse International brought home the point. He notes:

> *It became clear that people who prepare the ads are young art directors with eyes like eagles, and people who read the ads are 40, 50, and 60.*

BUSINESS-TO-BUSINESS ADVERTISING

The products in business-to-business and trade advertising are often abstract—financial services, healthcare, technology—and difficult to visualize. If your advertisement is running in aeronautic magazines that have nothing but photos of airplanes, think about *not* showing an airplane. Look for fresh solutions rather than settle for clichés.

Avoid "just as, so too" approaches.

The magazine is a farm journal. The visual is a boxing glove. The headline suggests that just as the glove knocks out opponents, so too the product gets rid of tough weeds.

This is lazy creative. Work harder to understand the target audience and their interests. A side-by-side comparison of your brand's potency versus another product would be more effective.

Stretch to find a compelling (and original) visual.

Don't settle for a forced visual or verbal link such as "Choose XYZ and get off on the right foot," with a foot as visual or a gushing faucet with the headline "Stop pouring money down the drain."

CFM International, a maker of jet engines, announced that its new engine consumed less fuel. The imaginative artwork showed a cactus in the shape of a plane. The headline: "To flourish in the current climate, you need to drink less."

Look for a storytelling illustration you are not likely to see in your competitor's ads.

Don't fall back on faces.

A frowning face to indicate a problem, a smiling face to show a solution. These are among the clichés that crop up often in business-to-business print advertising. Next time you are asked to approve a new layout, ask yourself if you are likely to see a similar visual running in the same magazine. If the answer is yes, tell the creative team to try harder.

Reading is active. You have to turn pages, focus on symbols, and convert them to thoughts and ideas. Reading takes energy, attentiveness, and absorption. Readers are therefore highly selective about the advertisements they choose to read.

HOW TO CONTROL PRINT PRODUCTION COSTS

Digital technology has revolutionized print production. If the photograph you want to use is in final form, you can create a four-color ad within 24 hours, including instant satellite delivery to the selected publications.

Art directors can try out 80 typefaces in 20 minutes, make a headline look like it's on a chalkboard or floating in water, change all the colors in a photograph. Instead of the old painstaking "kerning" with an Xacto knife to reduce space between letters, they simply instruct the computer.

A "rough" or "comp" print ad is surprisingly close to the finished product. The visual is likely to be a computer-generated version of the final photography or artwork. The headline, and probably the body copy, is set. (Occasionally, you will see text that is "Greeked in," which means it is set in nonreadable type, simply to indicate length.)

However, not everything in print production is immediate. The experts say that if a photography shoot is involved, because of several time-consuming steps, you should allow nine weeks for the entire process.

Costs have increased dramatically. Everyone knows it's essential to get a written estimate for a television commercial, because so much money is involved. Unfortunately, this step is too often ignored when it comes to print production. Clients who don't even blink at a $500,000 TV production bid are thunderstruck to find a print shoot, including purchase of photos, can easily run $200,000 or more.

Insist on a written estimate that itemizes costs. Equally important, ask for *revised* estimates in writing. Anything out of the ordinary should be a red flag for increased costs. This includes a "name" photographer or elaborate set construction, night or weekend shooting, use of children or animals (which can take forever) or special visual effects.

You may need expert guidance in business dealings with the photographer—especially one in the top echelon. Usually—unless you agree on a buyout—the photographer retains the rights to all the images completed on a given shoot. You or the agency can buy one or more photos for a specific run—identified media within an identified time period. If you decide later that you'd like to use that shot in a medium you have not bought, such as sales promotion or the internet, you need to negotiate with the owner—the photographer.

Another way to save production money is to ask yourself if you really need four-color ads, full pages, or spreads.

Jack Daniel's Tennessee Whiskey created one of the best-known brands in the world with two-third pages in black-and-white.

The best way to save money on print production may be the same as that offered in the chapter on television—create fewer, *better* ads, and run them for a longer time.

10 Radio and Outdoor

While it may seem surprising to talk about these two media together, they have several important things in common.

- *They both talk chiefly to an audience on the move.*
- *Both can deliver a large number of impressions even with limited dollars.*
- *Both are local and targeted.*

Before you create advertising for either radio or outdoor (which has grown as "out-of-home"—in airports, bus shelters, taxicab roofs, and almost everywhere else), form a mental picture of what your audience is doing when they receive the message. They are almost always doing something else at the same time.

RADIO—THE ONE-ON-ONE MEDIUM

Radio is a very *private* experience. We usually listen to radio alone—in our bedrooms while dressing, in our cars driving to and from work, on headsets while jogging.

Radio was predicted to sink under before a long list of technology advances—first TV, then tape decks and CD players in cars. Yet it maintains a solid base in car listening (talk radio, sports). There are more than 13,000 local stations in the U.S.—many markets have more than thirty stations. Radio is still the medium of choice for people to get their local news, weather, and traffic—the total morning audience rivals prime time TV.

Radio continues to go counter to our sound bite culture by selling 60-second lengths—twice as long as the usual TV spot. Copywriters find the length unwieldy. "I feel like I'm sitting down to write *Gone with the Wind,*" one complained. Yet try to buy a 30-second spot, and most radio stations will charge 80 percent of the full minute rate. Many advertisers feel that's a waste of money and buy :60s, when they might get sharper, more single-minded creative work with the shorter length.

We spend more time with radio than with any other medium—over 20 hours a week, according to the Radio Advertising Bureau. But we are not really *listening* the whole time. The radio is just there as comforting background sound.

There are dozens of different formats—all-news, all-talk, all-sports, classical, adult contemporary, country, rock, alternative, urban, religious—and most of these have subdivisions. Rock alone splits into classic rock, contemporary rock, hard rock, and more, each with its own fans. Programming manuals list over 140 different program types. There are stations for ethnic groups and for many different nationalities—one station in Detroit broadcasts programs in 21 different languages.

Some Principles of Radio Advertising

1. Focus on one idea. With no pictures to rivet them, listeners are easily distracted. Faced with filling 60 seconds, copywriters often add extraneous information. Be direct and clear. Make sure you are communicating the key consumer benefit.

The Boston Museum of Science drove home its promise—it could make even complex scientific subjects appealing to children. The Museum's radio commercial features a child singing "Itsy-Bitsy Spider," but with a new set of lyrics. "The itsy-bitsy arachnid went up the water spout. Down came the condensed atmospheric vapor and drove the arachnid out . . ."

2. Think about the program environment. The same commercial can be more or less effective when heard in different contexts. Many advertisers create spots with different musical styles suited to the different program formats—rock for rock stations, country for country stations, and so on.

However, you can often grab the listener's attention by *counter-programming*—creating a spot that deliberately cuts against the grain of the station's format.

Hofstra University wanted to reach high school juniors during the summer just before their senior year, to encourage them to apply to Hofstra. Instead of the more expected rock track, the school cast a serious, almost professorial spokesman who provided five little-known but compelling facts about Hofstra. The spot drew a record number of applications.

3. Don't splinter your efforts. If radio is supporting your television advertising, consider using some elements of your TV campaign—especially music.

Budweiser successfully transferred its television campaign to radio with spots that featured conversations between lizards that reminded listeners about aspects of the TV campaign, such as "born on" dating. The memorable voices of the lizards vividly recalled the television commercials.

4. Stretch the listener's imagination. Voices and sounds can evoke pictures, create atmosphere. They can transport people wherever you want them to go.

Little Caesar's launched its new, almost three-foot long "Pizza by the Foot" by describing a family eating away at its two ends. They converse in shouts. "Pass me a slice with pepperoni," the father yells to the son, who replies with a fast ball. "Boy, has that kid got an arm," Dad comments approvingly.

5. Register your brand name. They can't see it, so be sure that they hear it. Research studies say that you have the best shot of registering your brand name if you introduce it within the first ten seconds.

A dutiful son takes his mother out for a Sunday dinner at a prim and proper restaurant, which she compares over and over again to the better food and drinks atmosphere of Chili's, a Mexican restaurant chain. This commercial manages to mention the brand name, in an engaging way, six times, most of them right at the start.

6. Use the strength of music. Music can evoke feelings and emotions without the help of pictures. You can use the track from your TV commercial or something created just for radio. If you are relying on the lyrics to communicate your message, make sure your listeners can understand them. People under 35 can understand intricate, rapid lyrics—people over 40 may not.

7. Advertise promotions. No wonder retail stores are the biggest advertisers on radio. The medium is perfect for advertising and promoting national as well as local brands. "*This week only!*" works.

Consider live-delivery commercials—scripts read by the

program host, to capitalize on his or her credibility and personality.

Radio stations are usually eager to work with advertisers on contests, events, sampling, and live remotes. They are flexible and open to new ideas.

To reach its 21- to 28-year-old audience, Tuaca, an Italian liqueur, decided to put almost its entire advertising budget into radio. Its agency created a two-minute music program, "Tuaca Time."

Local restaurants and clubs could send in details of upcoming promotions and events, which were announced by the deejay host. Sales in "Tuaca Time" markets increased as much as 197 percent.

8. Listen to the commercial in context. Most listeners will not hear your commercial through a powerful studio audio system, nor will they be paying rapt attention. Play the tape or CD in your own car, knowing that people in the listening audience will be driving or reading or talking rather than just listening.

9. Make it topical and timely. Radio commercials are relatively inexpensive and quick to produce. Take advantage of this by being topical and relevant to the season, time of day, station format, and listener.

If it's near April 15, offer tax advice. If it's cold outside, sell hot beverages or antifreeze. If it's Friday, suggest something for the weekend. If the pollen count is high, sell decongestants. If it's morning, sell coffee to get listeners going.

"The best part of waking up is Folger's in your cup."

Drive time is an obvious opportunity to talk about cars, transmissions—and cell phones. Researchers find that drivers remember a commercial better than listeners at home.

 10. Talk one-to-one. Nobody does radio better than Motel 6, scripted and delivered by Tom Bodett, who speaks with candor to the business traveler or vacationer who is interested in a no-frills room for the night.

In one spot, Bodett urges his listeners to stop being "tube turnips," to get away from their TV sets and enjoy the spring weather. "Admire the vegetation instead of being part of it."

At the end of the day, he continues, you can call Motel 6 and get a "clean, comfortable room for around 24 bucks most places, a lot less in some, a little more in others. Always the lowest prices of any national chain." He closes with a reassurance to anyone who might suffer from an attack of the VTs—Video Tremens—to relax, because all Motel 6 rooms have free TV.

Every spot ends—as they have for the past decade and more—with the friendly line: "We'll leave the light on for you."

OUT-OF-HOME—THE *EVERYWHERE* MEDIUM

Out-of-home is defined as advertising that reaches consumers anywhere that is not their home or their office. We have been accustomed to thinking of this medium as larger-than-life outdoor advertising, like highway posters, that talks to large numbers of people at the same time, for the most part in quick takes.

Today, however, out-of-home is *everywhere*. No medium puts advertising messages before our eyes so constantly, in so many unexpected places and unusual ways.

Monster.com mowed a 500-foot-diameter crop circle with its logo directly below the flight path of Chicago's O'Hare airport.

CareerBuilder.com bought space on tops *of buses so job-seeking executives could look down from their offices and get the message.*

"Street Furniture"—the term for ads found in places like bus shelters and telephone kiosks—is proliferating. You'll find digital screens in office elevators, supermarket checkout lines, ATMs, gas station pumps, and public toilets. A beach-cleaning machine stamps out logos in the sand. A taxi-top medium receives signals from satellites to display only messages specific to a given part of town. Entire buildings can be painted, construction sites become marketing events, and the wrapped bus penetrates into affluent neighborhoods. Take a closer look at the egg you're boiling, the clothes you're wearing, or the suitcase you're traveling with—chances are somebody's logo is stamped on them.

Out-of-home is ubiquitous.

Outdoor Boards

This section is dedicated primarily to the big outdoor billboards or posters you see on highways. Creative people agree this is probably the most difficult medium of all—you have no more than seven seconds to deliver your message.

When asked to come up with a multimedia campaign that involves television, print, radio, and outdoor, creative director Steve Lance of Unconventional Wisdom always asks his troops to tackle outdoor first. "Once you get the poster right, everything else is easy."

Here are some things you can do to make sure your board gets the message across.

1. Look for a big, simple idea. Outdoor is a bold medium. Try for a "visual scandal" that delivers the idea quickly and memorably.

Posters are the art of brevity—one visual and no more

 than six or seven words, preferably fewer. In fact, research confirms that the most successful billboards are nonverbal. Cut out all extraneous words and pictures. Concentrate on essentials.

Apple uses towering, dramatic photos of contemporary figures—Einstein, Picasso, Muhammad Ali—who have changed our world. The posters simply display the Apple logo and the words "Think Different."

It pays to "break out of the box" and extend the poster beyond its borders. (This is more expensive, but can be well worth it.)

Chick-Fil-A, a restaurant chain that specializes in chicken, uses three-dimensional cows to drive home its message. In one poster, a cow stands on the back of another to paint, in bold, misspelled letters: "Eat Mor Chikin."

Crop your photographs to "heroic" proportions. Instead of a full-length figure, show just the upper body or the head. Even better, show only the eyes.

2. Use bold lettering and primary colors. Copy must be at least 12 inches high to be read at 100 feet. Avoid delicate typefaces, such as script.

Primary colors are more visible than pastels, with black on yellow the winning combination. Use daylight fluorescent color with care—it increases impact, but can create a circus effect.

Never rely on your own judgment or that of your art director to decide if your poster can be easily read and understood from a distance. Most outdoor companies have devices that simulate what your ad will look like 100 feet away or more.

3. Localize. Nothing beats the power of outdoor to lead tourists driving through town to your restaurant, store, or attraction.

Don't overlook the impact on the trade. The local supermarket manager may never see your commercials on TV, but will notice a big poster across the street from the store.

If you know that commuters drive by your site every day, you can create an attention-getting story.

> *The Western Insecticide Company of Spokane put up a big wooden poster that proclaimed: "There are no termites in Spokane." Every week, for the next several weeks, the poster changed, as the words were increasingly nibbled away. The last posting had only the word "Burp." And the name and telephone number of the exterminator.*

Attention-getting outdoor like this can also cause fender dents and get you noticed by the local media.

4. Look for human, emotional content. Remember that travelers are very often tired or bored. This is one medium where humor is truly welcome.

> *Jack Daniel's Tennessee Whiskey shows the big, familiar bottle and the words: "Made in a dry county. Go figure."*

5. Think direct marketing. Many advertisers report that it pays to include their 800 number and web site on every poster. For telephone numbers, it helps to give consumers words they can associate with the product, like 800-OK-Cabl, instead of just numbers.

6. Announce news. You can reach a huge percent of a market in the first day, according to Nielsen. For instance, 500 carefully placed posters in Los Angeles will be seen by most prospects the day they go up.

Altoids mounted a successful marketing campaign using telephone kiosks to introduce their breath mint into markets as difficult as New York. One of their first posters showed a bare-chested bodybuilder, posing with the package. The headline: "Nice Altoids."

Considering the success shown by Altoids (outdoor), and Motel 6 and Tuaca (radio), perhaps more advertisers should consider the impact and persuasion of these media when used creatively as *primary* advertising vehicles.

HOW TO CONTROL OUTDOOR PRODUCTION COSTS

Advertisers no longer have to worry about the endless paste and paper problems that used to plague outdoor. Computer imaging and reproduction make even photographic renditions breathtaking. (No wonder high fashion is another growing category.) Vinyl makes your poster look good longer.

Location, location, location are the first three real estate principles. Billboards in high-traffic locations like Sunset Boulevard or Times Square cost more. And prime space may well be held by one canny advertiser for years and years. But shop around. You might find a fire sale.

In other chapters, planning ahead is offered as one of the keys to keeping production costs in check. Nowhere is this advice more important than out-of-home advertising. You need to allow time for printing, for shipping, and for posting. All in all, you need four months from approval of creative idea to having your poster up on the highway.

The rule-of-thumb, then, is that to have an outdoor advertisement in place for July Fourth, you should be looking at creative executions by Groundhog Day—five months in advance.

11 The Internet

Marketers have been experimenting with interactive media since the late 1970s—first through the television set (videotext), then through electronic shopping systems and electronic information services (CompuServe). These were little more than experiments, offered to a handful of technically oriented users.

Then a British physicist named Tim Berners-Lee formulated many of the elements that today make up the basic foundation for the world wide web by creating a publishing "standard" around which anyone in the world could create and place an electronic publication on the internet.

Berners-Lee created the Big Bang that changed the world.

By the mid-1990s the number of internet users climbed from a few hundred thousand to more than 40 million, making it the fastest growing medium of all time. The distinguishing factor between the world wide web and all of the systems that preceded it was that Berners-Lee created an open standard. In other words, no single entity controlled the web. So long as users applied Berners-Lee's relatively simple system of creating and linking web pages, anyone could publish on the internet and anyone with an internet connection and a free program called a "browser" could read web pages.

The rest is history. The world wide web is now used in every corner of the globe—in homes, offices, and schools. Whether the internet will become a major advertising medium remains to be seen. However, investments on the web are growing, and it is becoming a part of media planning.

The internet is not merely another "medium," says Jeff Lanctot of the Avenue A agency, but it's also a "channel." "Customers aren't just viewing ads online, they're e-mailing customer service to ask about their new computer, researching automobile purchase, shopping for new clothes, and buying stereo equipment. For sophisticated marketers, the internet is not just a new place to advertise. It's also a new way to identify and engage customers."

HOW TO ADVERTISE ON THE INTERNET

For a time in the late '90s, some thought that the internet would totally revolutionize marketing. A "New Economy" would sweep away the past. We now see there is one economy—the one of profit-and-loss, and that the internet is an important part of that.

There are some who believe that the internet is not a branding medium. This misses the point. *Every* communication contributes to the brand image. Studies have long shown that media combinations have greater impact than any individual medium on its own, and there is now ample research to show that internet advertising can have very powerful branding effects.

Unilever tested internet advertising effects on four brand measures for Dove Nutrium Bar—unaided awareness, aided awareness, knowledge of brand attributes, and purchase intent. Published results indicated that the combination of print, TV, and online advertising increased brand measures more than TV only, print only, or TV plus print.

When the web first started, every advertiser wanted a giant web site. Fine if your customers need information from you prior to purchase (Ford), have intensive customer service needs (American Express), or buy your product online (Dell). Not so fine if the site ends up an exercise in vanity publishing and millions of dollars wasted (almost every packaged goods site).

Same is true with banners and pop-ups. Some advertisers have had enormous success with pop-ups (Orbitz) and banners (IBM), while others have chosen to experiment with their own content (BMW). The fact is, the medium is still in its infancy and advertisers will continue to experiment with new forms and approaches.

Despite the hype of the dot-com era, we now know that internet advertising shares one major attribute with all other forms of advertising—it builds brands and it sells products. The most important thing is to integrate your internet advertising with your overall brand strategy. And give it time and attention on the creative side.

In an internet age, it often seems that technology drives the message. Don't let technology get in the way of communicating with the consumer.

The IBM turnaround in the '90s was based on refocusing the company outward—on the pragmatic benefits of internet technology to IBM's corporate customers. "Tell me what it means to the customer," Lou Gerstner told his troops when he was CEO. "Don't talk to me about bandwidth or browsers, or that sort of stuff."

We've also learned a few things through all the trials and tribulations of this volatile new medium. Here are ten things to think about when creating an internet campaign:

1. Make your online advertising consistent with your offline strategy. One of the most commonly made mistakes in using interactive media is to treat it as a "one-off" medium, divorced from the positioning and messaging used offline. Treat your online campaign as a direct extension of your offline one.

- *To introduce its new C-class Mercedes, DaimlerChrysler used interactive media to help reach a younger audience with information, sweepstakes, and a call-to-action to visit a dealer. The interactive campaign extended the look and feel of the offline campaign, but succeeded in spreading the word to a new segment.*
- *Model Christy Turlington appeared in a series of public service announcements on television and in print to promote the idea that "smoking is ugly." This idea was successfully extended to the web through a new site featuring the model and offering a range of informative resources, an interactive quiz, and links to other antismoking web sites.*
- *The strategy for Memorial Sloan-Kettering Cancer Center—to encourage patients to come to* MSKCC first, *rather than for a second opinion—is carried over from print to the internet with a banner: "Just diagnosed with a brain tumor? We're ready to help."*

The web offers many new ways to interact with customers, making it all the more important that an integrated view of the brand be maintained across every media platform.

2. Use content and search sites to extend your brand campaign and reach your target audience. Just as advertisers use traditional media to help build brands, many have now turned to the internet to support their brands as ever-increasing numbers of consumers spend time online.

> *For decades Tiffany & Company has "owned" the franchise position on the upper right-hand corner of page three of* The New York Times. *As* The Times *extended its brand onto the web, Tiffany followed by buying the position next to the newspaper's flag on the home page.*

Often, consumers turn to search engines like Google to find information about a particular topic. Advertisers should use these search points to get information to people who are most interested in the category.

> *When AstraZenica, the pharmaceutical giant, launched an ulcer drug called Nexium, they made sure to buy "presence" on search engines whenever anyone typed in "heartburn." That way, consumers who were most interested in finding more about the relevant category would be introduced to the new drug.*

3. Define success. Don't expect the internet to miraculously solve all of your marketing problems. Clearly define what you want to achieve and attempt to develop the appropriate measure of success. If your basic objective is to get a consumer to enter your web site, the "click-through rate"—the percentage of users who go from your display ad on a content site into your web site—is the right measure. Otherwise, develop success measures that match your marketing objectives.

Many advertisers are finding that click-through, while the easiest and most obvious thing to measure online, fails to meet real success criteria. The most valuable asset that an advertiser has is the *brand*.

As interactive marketing becomes more mainstream, advertisers increasingly need to understand its effects on awareness levels, message association, purchase intent, and advertising recall. Research firms such as Dynamic Logic have come into existence to analyze marketing effectiveness—not simply measure "click-throughs"—for advertisers and their agencies.

Before you spend a single dime on interactive media, think about what you want to achieve.

4. Find content sites that attract your target audience. Users of internet content sites often visit them at work. They are focused on the content, not on your advertising. In order to get noticed, your message must be relevant. This is as true on the web as it is in any other medium.

The beauty of the web is in its infinite diversity. You can reach the entire online population or find only fly fisherman who like to fish in South America. If you're selling high-end consulting services, identify web sites populated by CEOs and other C-level executives. If you're selling high-end servers, intercept internet users when they're looking at technology reviews for your competitors' products.

Jim Warner, president of interactive advertising firm Avenue A/NYC, recommends thinking about reach on the web from three distinct perspectives.

Broad-based banner or "pop-up" campaigns—to reach the mass web audience. Advertisers can literally blanket the web by placing banners on hundreds of sites that reach almost every user during a given month. These banners can be bought at very low rates, usually on a cost-per-thousand basis. The purpose of this "B-52 campaign" is neither to selectively target, nor to create a special experience. It is merely to reach the broadest possible group of internet users at the lowest possible cost.

To quickly build awareness and traffic for its service, online travel agent Orbitz bought "pop-unders"—ads that appear on visitors' screens without their knowledge, behind the main content they are viewing—on sites across the internet. While users complained of the intrusion, the company found the campaign to be highly effective in driving new users to the site.

Targeting by content—to find users who may need specific information about a particular topic area. Typically, the cost of such targeting is higher than the mass approach, but the returns can also be higher.

Subaru targets users who are seeking Subaru-related information, including information about specific competitors. By using Edmunds.com to find consumers who may be about to purchase a car within Subaru's competitive set, the manufacturer can pinpoint a specific message designed to influence behavior.

Targeting by demographics or behavior—to find users who fit a particular profile or have a demonstrated interest in a particular category.

Amazon builds extensive behavioral profiles on its customers so that it can reach users with messages of particular relevance. For example, by tracking book or music preferences, Amazon sends e-mails to its customers when similar releases hit the marketplace.

5. **Make a compelling offer.** Part of what you may want to achieve online is a list of qualified leads. Similar to direct

 mail, offer a compelling reason for users to respond. Otherwise, they won't.

- *Adidas developed a special contest for users of ESPN.com. Visitors enter to win a round of golf with Ernie Els or Sergio Garcia. When they click to enter, they can get more information on Adidas golf shoes.*
- *Users were invited to click on a Hewlett-Packard banner to find out how to receive a "free business builders kit" when they purchase an All-in-One printer. The offer, targeted to small business owners, created a compelling call-to-action aimed at a specific segment of the web.*

Much of the value in internet marketing is in the notion of "opting-in"—a term that simply means giving an advertiser information in return for some benefit. The more upfront marketers are in this exchange, the less they will be prone to criticism about violating consumers' privacy rights.

Yahoo! was criticized for automatically enrolling its visitors in a program where they received e-mail without opting in. Many internet users consider this type of e-mail to be "spam," and either ignore it or delete it.

6. Minimize gimmickry. There is much gratuitous, annoying animation in web advertising. Use animation and interactivity, but as a part of the story. Your advertising needs to get noticed, but not at the expense of your brand. You cannot annoy the consumer into buying your product or service.

Lancôme built its beauty recommendation tool into a large-format banner. Users encounter the banners on content sites and enter their personal information to get tailored advice from the company. A good example of interactive branding.

Too many web users find internet advertising to be distracting. This is true principally because the creative work is crying to be noticed instead of telling a story important to the user at that time.

7. Sessions, not impressions. As in other forms of advertising, frequency is an important part of driving the message home. Too much internet advertising is aimed at undifferentiated "impressions"—not at specific users. Try to find sites that can target individual users. That way, you can buy a user "session" that allows you to "own" that user during an entire visit to the web site. You can develop an ongoing relationship with the user, developing real frequency.

8. Don't be afraid to experiment with your own content. The internet is a new medium. It is too early to set rules and define exactly what works and what doesn't. Advertising on content sites is fine, but there are other approaches.

To position itself as an exciting brand, BMW hired award-winning movie directors to create its own web content in the form of "BMW Films." BMW received enormous media coverage and many creative awards, and created tremendous "buzz" among its target. Best of all, this "experiment" was strategic, since BMW knew that some 80 percent of its purchasers visited the internet to receive automotive product information.

Don't make the mistake of believing that the consumer has a natural interest in your product or service. Companies have spent millions developing web sites that amount to little more than vanity publishing. If you do intend to invest heavily in your own content, make sure it's consistent with your brand position and is interesting enough to compete with the millions of other web sites on the internet.

Some advertisers have developed "micro-sites," usually in cooperation with a publisher, to link their brands with related, compelling content. The micro-site is typically promoted from the publishing partner's web site, providing not only content, but promotion as well.

9. Privacy pays. The number one fear that users have about online marketing is that their personal information, particularly credit card data, will be compromised. For this reason, it is very important to have a clearly identified privacy policy stating that private information will never be sold or transferred to a third party without the user's permission.

If you bring users to a web site where you expect them to enter personal information, make sure that your visitors can easily find your privacy policy.

10. Promotions work online. There's nothing like a promotion to engender short-term sales results. But the best promotions can do that and emphasize a point about the brand as well.

> *American Express is always looking for ways to offer advantages for Cardmembers. By aggregating many of its retail partners into an online "offer zone," the company enhances its business partnerships, offers the consumer a benefit (e.g., free shipping) that only Cardmembers can receive, and provides a promotional vehicle leading to increased sales. A win all the way around.*

You might think that only the giants of e-commerce can effectively play the selling game online. Not so. By applying the simple rules outlined above, even the smallest business can extend its reach and develop new markets.

The Jacob Burns Film Center, a suburban New York not-for-profit independent movie theater, has a successful e-commerce site. Customers can easily go onto the web, find out what's playing, and order tickets to assure a seat during busy performances.

CUSTOMER SERVICE—IDEALLY SUITED TO THE WEB

The web was not designed to be a customer service medium, but it is ideally suited to being one. Its proper use creates a highly effective relationship with your best clientele.

Make it easy for your internet visitors to get information or take action.

Your customers often need access to content that only you can provide, everything from your hours of business to specific descriptions of your product and services. Think about all the questions these folks have about your business. Outline them. This can serve as a basic "map" that any web developer or consultant can use to create an efficient channel between you and your visitors.

Under the headline "Have your online purchases shipped with Priority Mail," the United States Postal Service offered a simple link to click: "I want to tell my online retailer about Priority Mail."

Under the headline "Tell your online retailer you want it shipped Priority Mail," the USPS link was "I want to send my online retailer this e-mail."

Your customers share a passion for your brands.

Open up a way for them to share their stories—good and bad—about your products. Allow them to answer questions and help one another. One of the things that Steve Case did very well in building America Online was to treat his customers as a community. AOL customers still help one another answer questions about how to use the service, as they did when it first started in the mid-'80s.

Use e-mail to solve problems.

A cigar smoker ordered a humidor from a small site called American Crafts Online. When it came, there were no instructions about how to create the right level of humidity. He e-mailed this question. In return, a fellow named Charles Tedder, the craftsman who actually carved the humidor, sent him a personal e-mail along with instructions and the URL for his web site, where he could get more information. Now that's customer service.

Support direct sales with enhanced services.

We've already discussed basic principles about selling online. But customer service can go beyond direct sales:

Barnes & Noble, the book superstore, allows shoppers on its web site to return items to its stores. This is a great example of how a bricks-and-mortar business can help customers who shop online.

Put the customer in the center of the universe.

All of the aspects of your relationship with the consumer come together in the way you design your web site. Nowhere is this more evident than on your home page, which is like the front door to your business. Is it welcoming? Is it a place where your customers want to spend time? To interact? To look for information? To get the services they need? Or is it a useless PR device with little or no value offered?

The web site is the first medium to allow the smallest business to interact with customers all over the world. From "talking" directly with the fellow who carved your humidor to returning a book that you bought online to a store in your neighborhood, the web builds bridges that could never be built before.

Make sure your customers can find you.

If you manage a major consumer brand, most customers will be able to find your site simply by typing your name into the URL format. For example, if you're interested in information from Ford, chances are you're savvy enough to type *www.ford.com* into your browser.

But most companies are not as recognizable as Ford. Perhaps you own a small business, or are launching a new brand. Often, consumers will search for a company by typing a category—such as "hotels in Paris"—into a search engine like Google. Fifty-five percent of all e-commerce transactions originate from a search listing. How can you be found in the vast ocean of internet choices? How can you make sure that your site will rank near the top of all listings when a consumer does an online search?

One way is to buy "search terms"—sometimes called "sponsored links" or "paid listings"—on the most popular search engines. A search term is simply a word ("hotels") or short phrase ("business consultant") that a user might enter into a search engine. Think of it as a kind of electronic yellow pages. Typically, advertisers bid for search terms on a cost-per-click basis. This means that the advertiser only pays the search engine when the consumer clicks.

A second way to increase your chances of being found in a search engine is to use an "optimization" service.

 These are online media consultants who will help you work with search engines to move your ranking closer to the top of the search engine display screen. There are dozens of companies that can help you drive traffic to your web site.

A third way is to fully integrate your URL into your offline campaigns. Make sure that viewers of your print and broadcast advertising can see your URL.

INTERACTIVE ADVERTISING—A WORK IN PROGRESS

Despite growing pains, the internet is changing marketing. Advertisers are faced with ever-increasing numbers of consumers who have access to voluminous information, from competitive pricing data to comprehensive product reviews, at the touch of a few keystrokes. The playing field is leveling out. Gone are the days when the marketer holds all the cards in the transaction.

While this chapter has argued strenuously that the traditional rules of advertising strategy and brand management apply every bit as much to the internet as they do to all media, the internet is the one medium where the user is in complete control at every point of the experience.

Moreover, the internet is *measurable* in a way that other media simply are not. The advertiser has access to so much information about the consumer's usage pattern, the challenge is to separate the wheat from the chaff—to understand what matters to the marketer's branding and selling objectives. Just because something can be measured doesn't mean that it is important.

But perhaps the most important aspect of interactive media is that it exists in a world of constantly changing technology. Here are three technologies that will continue to have impact far into the future.

Anywhere, Anytime Computing

The continuing evolution of wireless services and portable devices leads us to a media environment where the consumer will have access to any form of information—audio, video, text, and photography—from any access point.

What might it mean when you walk into a retail store with a wireless device and the store "recognizes" you as a loyal customer? If you've "opted-in" to receive offers from that store or from manufacturers who supply that store, how will that change the way you shop?

> *You can now walk into most Starbucks coffee shops and access the internet through an instore wireless network. This can attract many more customers, who will now use the store as a place to work.*

The Broadband Internet

Many people now gain access to the internet through a *broadband* connection. Most of these people are accessing the net at work, but increasingly cable and telephone companies are offering high-speed access to home users.

Broadband creates new challenges for marketers. Use of so-called *rich media*—internet advertising that incorporates animation, sound, or video—has expanded dramatically. The balance between a user's desire to fully control the online experience and the advertiser's need to intrude on that experience in order to deliver a message is strained by the increasing use of ever-more intrusive media formats.

As high-speed access becomes the norm, consumers will "vote" with their time and attention to establish this balance.

The Networked Home

People who already have at least one PC are now the consumers who purchase most new PCs in the U.S. Just as automobiles were a rarity at the beginning of the twentieth century, and now have become ubiquitous (many Americans own *three* automobiles), so the PC has become a mass-market necessity.

Increasingly, American consumers are surrounding themselves with digital gadgets—one, two, and in some cases three PCs in the home, perhaps a notebook for the road, and a personal digital assistant (PDA) for scheduling and other tasks. Cellular phones are now incorporating access to the internet for e-mail and web access.

Add to these computing devices the reality that soon almost all of our cable and satellite receivers will be fully digital, capable of storing and sending all kinds of information across the internet.

All of this leads inexorably to the networked home, where all of one's digital devices are connected to one another and to the internet. How advertising will be produced, bought, targeted, and distributed in this environment is unfolding. But if we have learned anything from the internet, it is that consumers hunger to connect with the companies and brands they love.

Consumers have always wanted more information. Now, in this era, we have the technology to deliver it. And they will decide whether to use it or delete it.

12 Direct Marketing

Why do more people now do their shopping by catalog or online?

The fastest-growing communications discipline, direct marketing was first propelled by sophisticated computer models, better databases, and new technologies such as the internet, mobile phone, and digital TV. Increasingly busy lifestyles and a deteriorating in-store experience accentuated this trend. Salespeople have become more invisible and cash register lines longer while improved support from direct marketers has enhanced the convenience of shopping from home or office.

Not just convenience but service. Online booksellers know your taste and recommend books you might like, wrap and send presents—and there are no lines. Floral services remind you of birthdays and anniversaries, and what you gave last year.

Direct marketing is any activity whereby you communicate directly with your prospect or customer, and he or she responds directly to you. The joy of direct marketing is its accountability—you quickly know the exact results of an advertising investment.

The ability to market directly to an individual or business with increasing precision derives from new analytical tools to create proprietary databases and mailing lists enriched with information about an individual or family beyond the address. Database marketing takes the medium to a new level by increasing the ability to match a product and message with a person's proclivity to buy. It has become more important to reach the right people than to reach more people.

Coupons to clicks

Direct marketing has evolved to include everything from directly selling to consumers to building long-term relationships with customers—with reward programs, multi-channel communications programs and the use of sophisticated CRM (Customer Relationship Management) software to track customer transactions. It has gone far beyond the late-night direct response TV spot or junk mail and now includes highly sophisticated work in every medium. Everything from coupons to clicks, as direct marketing pro Jerry Pickholz puts it.

Contemporary direct marketing, says industry pioneer Lester Wunderman, is relationship marketing. In his words:

> *What we are selling are not products, or even services, but ongoing relationships between suppliers of services or products and their individual users. Relationships require a dialogue. They can't exist without one.*

No matter the medium or the objective, the core principles remain the same.

IT PAYS TO TEST

The secret of successful direct marketing is in knowing what has worked and challenging those results with new testing every time.

> *We learn the principles and prove them by repeated tests. This is done through keyed advertising, by*

traced returns, largely by the use of coupons. We compare one way with many others, backward and forward, and record the results. When one method invariably proves best, that method becomes a fixed principle.

So wrote Claude Hopkins, the most successful copywriter of his era, in *Scientific Advertising* in 1923.

Today's testing still relies on tracking responses and sales. Now software programs and databases track and analyze all the different types of responses coming in—phone calls, coupons, online clicks, e-mails, web site registrations, "unsubscribe" requests, purchases, and other transactions.

It is common to find that one communication will produce many times the response of another for the same product.

A series of tests for a shopper's buying service included mailings to 12 lists, 3 prices, 2 ways to pay, different times for mailing, alternative ways to respond, and several creative approaches. The best combination of all these factors pulled 58 times better than the worst combination.

Testing the list can lift response ten-fold, notes David Kenney, Chairman/CEO of Digitas. He goes on to say testing the offer can deliver a five-fold increase and testing the creative can double the response—principles that adhere no matter what the medium.

You don't have to be big to test. In many cases, if you can generate 100 to 200 responses—enough for a statistically valid sample—you can get away with mailing as few as 10,000 pieces.

Don't assume anything. You will be surprised.

- *People will read long copy—it often pulls better than short.*

- *Some months (or even weeks or days) are more productive than others.*
- *Sometimes a higher price will produce more response than a lower one.*
- *People will respond again and again to the same mailing. Never change a successful mailing until you have a proven winner to replace it.*
- *It always pays to test if you plan to contact a substantial number of people, or if you plan to contact them more than once.*

Test

Test anything that could significantly increase response rates or decrease costs—copy, layout, colors, offers, terms, prices, premiums, lists, enclosures, the complete package or ad. Even fractional improvements year after year can make a substantive difference in profitability.

> *As* USA Today *used more e-mails for subscriptions, they experimented with formats. After trying many different colors, fonts, and layouts, they achieved a major lift by simply indenting the offer paragraph.*

Be careful with focus group sessions, which can be useful (or misleading) in generating hypotheses.

> *"My rule of thumb for direct response creative is, if it does well in groups, it fails in the mail. Most people will never admit to opening, much less responding, to the junk mail package or the spam e-mail or the direct response TV spot. Yet of course we know they respond in droves."*
>
> —HEATHER HIGGINS, CREATIVE DIRECTOR

It pays to verify qualitative research with quantitative studies.

Test only one variable at a time.
If you test several, you won't know which helped—or how much. Then combine all your winners and test again.
Watch what works in each medium. If a new offer works in the mail, it might work on TV, or on the web.

If you cannot test, take advantage of the testing of others. When you see the same DRTV spot or receive the same mailing over and over, year after year, you can be reasonably sure it has been proven in testing. Observe the mailings from Publishers' Clearing House, which uses cells of 100,000 people to test any changes. Note the long letters, read-outs, and multiple enclosures. PCH *knows.*

THE TRUE VALUE CONCEPT

To decide how much to invest in each potential customer, you must know or estimate how much each customer is worth—his or her "true value" over time.

It will almost always cost more to get a new customer than you will receive in an initial order. If you expect people to order something just once, the calculation is easy—will you get enough money to cover the cost of the merchandise and still make a profit?

Most direct marketing is in a different category. It goes to people who buy more than once. The object therefore is to get profitable names.

> *The New York Red Cross found that it paid to send first-time givers a free first-aid manual to convert them to donors, who were found to give in four of the following seven years, and increase their donations 20 percent.*

Repeat customers have measurable long-term, ongoing value, and it's far easier to sell something to the customer you have than to sell to a new customer. Many direct marketers find it profitable to solicit existing customers 10 to 12 times a year.

The basis for evaluation is cost efficiency against a marketing objective—not just the number of responses but the conversion rate from inquiry to sale. If you use only efficiency as the basis for all evaluations, you will end with the cheapest mail packages, not necessarily the most effective.

WHAT WORKS BEST IN DIRECT AND E-MAIL

With the caveats that one should assume nothing and that everything must be tested:

1. **Personalize and customize.** Databases and in-line printing presses allow us to personalize and customize communications more than ever. But be creative—effective personalization is much more than putting the correct name on the letter.

- *An effective mail package for the American Airlines AAdvantage credit card used the recipient's mailing address to calculate how many miles he or she could earn for their most frequent trips.*
- *Tesco, the leading supermarket in the UK, developed one of the most successful loyalty programs in the world. With the data collected for each member, Tesco was able to personalize mailings according to past purchases and life-stage. Over two million different variations of a direct mail piece were created.*

2. **Get to the point quickly.** Much direct mail is read over a wastebasket and e-mail with a finger on the delete button.

Open with a message that speaks to the reader in a very personal way.

"Quite frankly, the American Express Card is not for everyone. And not everyone who applies for Cardmembership is approved." This was the opening for a long-running mailing that beat all alternates in attracting new applications.

"Good direct mail flatters, intrigues, charms, cajoles," says direct marketing expert Drayton Bird, "but, above all, it gets to the point quickly, with news of benefits for the prospects."

Use the upper third of the e-mail—what shows in the preview window—to highlight key benefits and offers.

3. **Make sure the offer is right.** Other than the list itself, no element will make more of a difference than what you offer the consumer in terms of product, price, or premium.

The Economist *magazine offered subscribers three alternate renewal offers—with varying prices and number of weeks. Not surprisingly, the lowest price attracted the most subscribers. It also resulted in more conversions to full-price renewals and therefore the largest profit, despite the initial 40 percent reduction.*

Offers won't always work the same way in every medium. While discounted books are the mainstay of book clubs in direct mail and print, the web is another story.

While testing a variety of discounts by e-mail to prospect lists, Doubleday sent one group no discount at all. The no-discount group responded at a level 300 percent higher than the control. The perception among the offer-saturated web audience was that if there was a discount, the book wasn't very good. No discount implied a greater value.

Free is the most powerful offer you can make, but beware of attracting only one-time buyers.

4. Make the envelope or subject line work for you.

It was hard not to open an envelope with a cartoon captioned "I can't take all the credit but it was my decision to hire Kenneth Roman." The cartoon showed an executive with a sharply rising sales graph and introduced a special subscription offer from the Harvard Business Review.

The envelope is what people see first. Tease them. Tip your offer. Tell them about a gift inside, or about valuable information.

"Hurrah! Hurrah! London double miles extended to August 31" is the envelope opener for United Airlines.

5. Make it visually interesting. If you can afford only a brochure or a letter, send the letter, but help the reader with cross-heads (like "Make the envelope or subject line work for you."), handwritten read-outs, or inset paragraphs (like the Gevalia example—below).

The same principle works for e-mail, the electronic equivalent of a brochure. Use graphics, pop-ups, or other devices to pull the reader through.

6. Make sure the product is positioned correctly. A promise test can help decide the best positioning.

Gevalia coffee was positioned as the choice of real coffee lovers, because it is imported from Sweden, where people drink more coffee than anywhere else in the world.

7. Ask for the order. Every communication should ask for a response. Don't let prospects off the hook. Leave them with something to do, so they don't procrastinate. The web has made this easier than ever. Consumers seem to find it easier to visit a web site instead of calling. But be careful: sites are better at providing information than converting responders to buyers.

Some direct marketers believe in involvement devices like yes/no tokens. More useful are tangible reasons for action, like limited-time offers or some reward for replying quickly.

P.S. Don't forget to use the P.S. It is one of the best-read parts of a letter.

8. Cultivate an appropriate brand personality. A good letter or e-mail is appropriate to both the product and the audience.

> *A long-running letter from* The Wall Street Journal *talked about the twenty-fifth college reunion of two men who were very much alike and had gone to work for the same company. "But there was a difference. One of the men was manager of a small department of that company. The other was its president."*
>
> *The letter asks, "What made the difference?" It doesn't say that the* Journal *was the secret, but it does say, "The difference lies in what each person knows and how he or she makes use of that knowledge."*

Match the tone to the target audience and the subject.

> *To create a bond of trust with Taxoterre, a brand of chemotherapy for recurrent breast cancer, a program called "Living With It" provided information that went beyond the disease to help a woman deal with her entire life. The spokesperson, an agency copywriter and two-time survivor, wrote most of the program, drew the illustrations, and used her handwriting for the typeface.*

 9. Treat the customer as a friend. Don't resell a product to someone who is already using it. Maintain a consistent posture in treating the customer as a friend and in nurturing that relationship.

Jack Daniel's invited its best customers to become members of a club. It gave each of them one square foot of land in Tennessee, solemnly pronounced them Tennessee Squires, and proceeded to treat them like major landowners who would be interested in farm equipment auctions, plans for outhouses, even reports of poachers on their land. More recent e-mails to the Squires invite them to visit the home page on the internet.

A renewal letter should assume the customer likes the product and only needs a reminder. It can convey a sense of urgency or use a special offer as an incentive. *Flowers.com* sends e-mails reminding customers of anniversaries, birthdays, and other events (as requested).

Try to find original ways to let customers know you value them. Go beyond language to include small gifts, tokens, or thank you notes.

10. Integrate direct and e-mail with other communications. Maintain a common strategy and brand personality with everything that touches the consumer. When credit card companies change a campaign or launch a new promotion, everything is integrated down to the "Take One" applications found in restaurants.

To break out in newspapers that were exceptionally cluttered with competitive PC advertising, Compaq scheduled a special-offer ad that allowed them to "own" Tuesdays. Direct-mail postcards and e-mails alerted customers and prospects to look in USA

Today *on "Business Tuesdays" for high value offers.*

11. Be memorable. You cannot bore someone into loving you. Nor can your brand. Create communications and moments that are memorable.

- *To get through to the key community of senior people in the fashion industry, Lufthansa sent a mail package that took the form of a tailored shirt. The Lufthansa label was stitched in and a reply card was slipped into the pocket. Five contracts each worth $1 million followed.*
- *The United States Postal Service shipped boxes of apples to its most highly valued customers to demonstrate that comparing USPS rates to competitors just wasn't an "apples to apples" comparison.*

12. Repeat your winners. The most effective letter or e-mail—your control—is the standard. Try to beat it by adding something or modifying the offer. Or "down-test"—remove elements, such as a brochure, or find other ways to save money. Test every variable, but keep using the original until you find something better, and then make that your new control.

BROADCAST DIRECT MARKETING

Direct response advertising on TV or radio helps close sales, generate leads, or supplement advertising in other media. It has its own disciplines and principles.

- *Commercials should be as long as it takes to make the sale, often as long as the two-minute maximum. Few viewers can make a buying decision in less time than that. Also it takes time—as much as 30 seconds—to register the response number or ordering details.*

- *The best commercials set forth a problem, include a demonstration that shows why the product is the best solution, offer a money-back guarantee, and give the price—while asking for the order.*
- *There must be a sense of urgency, an offer or other reason to buy now: "Exclusive—not available elsewhere."*

Ryder built its share of the truck rental business with two-minute commercials that raised awareness of its expertise in this market. It offered do-it-yourselfers a step-by-step moving guide, a 10-percent discount on moving supplies, and a free Sony FM Walkman radio for responders who rented a Ryder truck.

Infomercials, also known as "long-form" television direct response advertising, are program-length (usually 30 minutes) spots that rely on documentary-type creative formats. They are particularly suited for products that are sold best by demonstration—exercise equipment, music CDs, cleaning devices, or other self-help products. Many mainstream advertisers are wary of infomercials, says expert Ron Bliwas, because some do not reflect the image they want to project.

TELEMARKETING

There are two telephone systems in direct marketing—inbound and outbound.

Inbound is the growing use of 800 (toll-free) numbers for placing an order from an advertisement or catalog and 900 (toll) numbers for buying a service—weather information, sweepstakes tickets, free order samples.

WATS Telemarketing was an integral part of the Ryder Truck Rental program. Calls generated a database of 150,000 prospective movers and their planned moving dates.

Outbound is the use of the phone to close a sale or offer a product or service. At its irritating worst, cold-calling is a controversial medium that is now beginning to regulate itself and limit both the hours calls are made and the tone of the call.

The voice on the telephone (and the script) is the closest thing to being in a store. On the phone, real people create the brand's image. With a well-trained staff and some self-restraint, telemarketing can be an effective and cost-efficient means of reaching people not reached elsewhere.

RELATIONSHIP MARKETING

The concept of building personal relationships with your most profitable customers is a timeless fundamental for success in business. In earlier days, the grocery store owner threw in a little free candy with the order. Today, your bank sends a thank you note through the mail. Or the web site sends you an e-mail with a special offer.

Thanks to sophisticated databases, enriched mailing lists, and a long history of learning from direct marketing, marketers are creating more personal and more effective relationship marketing programs than ever before.

Relationship marketing is less ambitious than customer relationship marketing (CRM), a way to manage customers, their transactions, and customer service interactions throughout an entire organization. Our reference here is direct marketing programs that tempt prospects and customers to have an ongoing relationship with a brand.

All relationships are personal. And creating them usually means bringing customers and companies together—whether on the phone, on the web, or in person.

IBM realized that the only thing holding them back from achieving targets in their European Netfinity division was the lack of relationships between themselves and the nine largest distributors, so they created the IBM Treasure Hunt.

Teams were invited to an outdoor adventure in Austria. Each team was sent a series of six direct-mail packages with personalized hints on where the IBM Gold Treasure was hidden. By the time they played the game along with their IBM teammates, the relationships had been transformed into personal partnerships.

Build a rich database.

The foundation of relationship marketing is the database—simply a list of best prospects, individuals or companies. The database is created by combining relevant information from several sources, exchanged with other companies that have similar profiles, or rented from list brokers.

The strategic use of customer information has two major thrusts. It reduces advertising waste by targeting marketing efforts to high-value prospects. It maximizes the value of each customer by building a relationship through continuous communications.

Success turns on how persuasive, relevant, and timely your messages are, says Drayton Bird, and this is determined largely by how you capture, store and use the right details. In his words:

You develop your database in the same way you develop your knowledge of other people. It starts as just names and addresses; each added scrap of information makes it more valuable. You overlay it with data already in the public domain or gathered by private enterprise.

With powerful information like this, a company can stay close to the customer—by mail, e-mail, fax, or phone. An integrated database program builds profitable relationships by continually updating information from customers and building it back into personalized messages or products. The more data included, the better the program. Delving into that database can lead to powerful insights about customers and revenue.

Hampton Inn used new analytic tools to examine their customer transaction database. Digging into the in-house database and matching those names with outside lists, they found that most of their revenue came from business travelers (single males on weekdays) rather than the leisure travelers (families) they'd been targeting, leading them to reassess their marketing program.

Assessing the potential revenue each customer could bring over the lifetime of the relationship is the first step to developing a profitable relationship marketing plan. Most companies find that 20 percent of customers generate about 80 percent of revenue. These should be the target for any relationship marketing efforts.

Database modeling showed that Clairol's best potential was among the one out of four U.S. women who buy hair color. By providing a large number of ways for customers to give personal information—web site registration, signing up for a newsletter, participating in a sweepstakes—it took only one year for Clairol to capture 50 percent of the most valuable customer names in its databases and to start seeing share shifts in its target audience.

Provide useful information.

Just sharing information with customers can make a relationship meaningful—especially when it's at an important life-stage.

A direct marketing program for Huggies disposable diapers targeted pregnant women, sending them informational mailings before their children were born, followed by timed mailings as the babies entered different stages of development (and diaper usage).

Kimberly-Clark then developed Parentstages.com, *a web site that brought together all their newborn and childcare brands to build relationships with expectant and new moms and dads. The site aggregated the best available content from respected partner sites, made it accessible in one place. It allowed Kimberly-Clark to learn about the target's particular interests and needs, and tailor information and offers accordingly.*

Create involvement.

Ask your customer's opinion about a product he or she has bought or one that you're developing.

Mercedes-Benz asked prospective customers who'd bought SUVs in the past what they liked and didn't like about their current vehicle. It reported the results as well as prototype test results for the new M-B SUV. A total of 73 percent of respondents stated they would consider buying the new vehicle.

Providing important customers with a lot of ways to be involved in your product or service can achieve a tight bond—if only because they're interacting with the brand many times over a period of time.

Touching the Customer

"Direct marketing is not always a cheaper way of marketing," says Drayton Bird. "When properly managed, direct marketing directs your efforts more accurately, giving you more for your marketing money."

That's why most advertising spending today goes to direct and relationship marketing. It is testable and accountable. It can market to different geographies, demographics, and affinity groups. Its learning permeates everything marketers do.

Touching the customer directly does more than create direct sales revenue. It creates trust between the customer and the brand, the single most important thing an advertiser can do to increase sales. The more people trust you, the more they will buy from you.

DIRECT MAIL FOR PROSPECTS, E-MAIL FOR RELATIONSHIPS

Prospecting for new customers is far better accomplished with direct mail. In one study, the cost per sale to a direct-mail prospect list was $73, the cost per sale to an online list was $1,250—despite the radically lower production and distribution costs.

E-mail is ideal for relationships with existing customers—highly effective and very low cost (assuming an up-to-date customer list). Open rates, click-through rates, offer-take rates, and response rates are all higher, and the cost per sale is lower.

How to execute in each medium is more similar than different.

DIRECT MAIL	E-MAIL
The envelope teaser is critical to getting opened.	The subject line is critical to getting opened.
Graphics are important to show the product and brand imagery.	Graphics are important. They differentiate you from spam, but need to be the right file size for recipients.
Integrate with advertising and brand communications.	Integrate with advertising and web site. E-mail graphics must integrate smoothly between advertising and web site to create a consistent brand experience.
Personalization lifts response, but its use is limited by cost and data availability.	Personalization and customization are expected by customers, who are well aware they've given you information.
Get to the point. People read their mail over the trash can.	Get to the point. Their fingers are on the delete button.
The number of mailings is driven by the lifetime value of the customer.	Because e-mail costs are low, it is tempting to e-mail often. E-mail too often, open rates go down.
Member-get-member pieces are occasionally effective.	A visible viral unit can be very effective—people pass them on to their friends.
Prospects require a lot of information to buy. Customers require less to make second or third purchases. But test!	Be brief to prospects (backed by an info-rich web site). Be information-rich to customers.
Success criteria—response, conversion to sale, cost per sale, total revenue per customer.	Success criteria by e-mail—open rate, click-through rate, how many filled out form or registered on web site, viral name acquisition, unsubscribe rate.
Put a call to action in the headline, the letter copy, and P.S., and the brochure and response device.	Put a call to action in the upper left-hand corner or in the preview window. Use multiple links throughout the e-mail, put another call to action at the bottom.

13 Brochures, Web Sites, Sales Pieces

Every business needs a sales piece—to make a connection with a consumer and close a transaction. Every consumer needs a sales piece to get a description of a product or service and enough information to be able to order something.

Brochures and catalogs were predicted to disappear, to be replaced by inexpensive videotapes, computerized information, and the ease of shopping on the internet. Not so! Whether consumers are buying a vacation or a car, they still like to thumb through a brochure. Catalog sales have been growing, as even habitual internet shoppers tend to browse through a catalog before buying.

As more people shop online, however, it is increasingly clear that every business needs a web site as well. They make sense for any business with a long product line or one that must be constantly updated. No catalog can show so many things as well as a web site, with color and detailed product specifications.

- *Brochures provide a feel and image of a product, place, or service.*
- *Catalogs add specific descriptions, including price, and the ability to order.*
- *Web sites can do both.*

Some sales pieces are clearly more effective than others—attracting more attention, inviting readers, and increasing sales. Others are a waste of time and money. Certain principles are similar to those for print ads. Many, however, are unique to sales pieces and can contribute greatly to effectiveness.

Advertising and sales pieces march to the same drummer. The visuals, words, and personality of the sales piece should flow from the positioning of your brand. If you are advertising in another medium, there should be some family resemblance.

Understand your target audience, and what they want. Study the competition and figure out where you might have an edge. Perhaps you can be preemptive by making a statement any competitor could make—except you end up owning it!

There are many hotels along New York City's Central Park South—all facing Central Park. For years, one hotel boasted, "Central Park is our front yard." It preempted the truth.

BETTER BROCHURES

1. Put your selling message on the cover. The cover of a brochure works like the headline of a print advertisement. State your position or promise a benefit to the reader.

The cover should tell the reader who you are, where you are, and what you are.

The Running Y ranch resort in Oregon knows that people today are under a lot of stress. Its cover simply shows tranquil mountain and lake scenery with the message "Refresh your soul."

2. Be single-minded. Many brochures fail because they try to show everything, tell everything, and be all things to all people. They end up with lots of postage stamp–size photographs and lengthy copy that speaks to many different audiences.

Try this discipline. If you had to choose only *one* photograph for the entire brochure, what would it be? If the penguin is hands-down the most popular attraction of your zoo, your selection is easy.

When choosing photos, don't overlook the obvious. Tourists still prefer the Eiffel Tower or Big Ben over more obscure photos.

3. Use a single illustration on the cover. Research says that one large illustration is more effective than several small ones. And illustrations with bright colors and story appeal involve the reader.

4. Always caption photographs. Captions are read almost twice as often as body copy, yet no more than one out of five brochures bothers to caption photos. Captions that give the reader lots of pithy information work harder than short, bland ones.

A brochure offering African safaris put this caption beneath the photo of an elephant mother and her baby: "With a gestation period of 22 months, the elephant delivers a single calf. Eventually weighing 6–7 tons, this giant pachyderm can charge at 25 m.p.h. Twice the circumference of its front foot equals its height."

5. Avoid clichés. Visual clichés abound in brochures. The smiling chef appears in every hotel pamphlet; the couple holding hands on a beach is a staple of travel pieces. Next time you are selecting photos, ask yourself if you are likely to see a similar shot in your competitor's brochure. If the answer is yes, *don't use it.*

Don't ever invite a photographer, even a star, to wander around and shoot at random. Take the time to draw up a detailed "shot list" of exactly what photos you want, what angle you want them taken from, even the time of day or night that shows them off to best advantage.

> *The marketing director of The Boulders resort knew that for a few brief moments, just before dusk, the sun splashed unique reflections on a particular rock. The photo made a spectacular cover. That was planning, not chance.*

Plan ahead. Don't wait until spring to discover you don't have any shots of your fall foliage.

6. Load it with facts. The most frequent criticism of brochures is that they don't give enough facts. Tell consumers what is included—the prices, hours, range of products or services. They want practical, helpful information—what the climate is like in your area, is a tie required in your hotel dining room, do you accept all major credit cards.

Design and write for the skimmers. Few people will read a brochure cover to cover, but they might skim the headlines and call-outs, or linger on the charts.

Consider including a special URL that links with your web site. This will let you update information and pricing, as well as capture qualified leads. The specific URL will allow you to track how much traffic came from the brochure.

7. Make your piece worth keeping. Brochures that unfold into posters suitable for framing are one good example. Designer Milton Glaser created dozens of collector's items for the "I Love New York" campaign. Yearly calendars of events also give your brochure a longer life.

8. Give your product or service a first-class ticket. Don't stint on quality. In many cases, the brochure *is* your product. If your budget is limited, consider a smaller mailer or a classy black-and-white piece instead of four-color. Another alternative is black-and-white plus one color. A black-and-white brochure can really pop out of a rack filled with four-color pieces.

9. Use the envelope to deliver a message. Tease the readers, whet their appetites, promise them a benefit for opening the envelope and reading on.

> *Colorado's Steamboat resort, a savvy marketer,* always *has something important on the envelope. One mailing to previous guests promised "Returning to Steamboat has its own rewards. Up to $200 worth. Details inside."*

10. Ask for the order. What action do you want the reader to take? Telephone, visit your web site, send a check? Every brochure should contain a clear call to action.

TRAVEL BROCHURES

The travel, tourism, and hospitality industries—including ski areas, theme parks, and attractions—are the heaviest users of brochures. They share a number of challenges—diffuse target audiences (business travelers, pleasure seekers, travel professionals); a need to present lots of information in one brochure; schizophrenic personalities (one benefit in high season, a different one in off-season.)

The most important principle is to identify an umbrella positioning and stick with it, for all audiences and all seasons.

Announcing news is helpful for travel and tourism—for amusements and attractions, it is lifeblood. Visitors are drawn to return by a promise of new adventures. The best place to announce news is on the cover. You can make the old cover last one more year by using an overlay or snipe.

WEB SITES

Almost since its inception, marketers have been using the web to provide comprehensive information about products and services. At first, these web sites were little more than replications of the print brochures and were derogatorily referred to as "brochure-ware" or "shovel ware," because they were not using the unique aspects of the web.

With more than half of all consumers now researching major categories of purchase such as travel and automotive online, creating an electronic brochure on the internet has improved dramatically. These sites can sometimes be less costly substitutes for printed documents while providing more comprehensive and personalized information.

The best internet sites allow users to quickly and easily get the information they want. Here are things to keep in mind when using the internet to either replace or supplement your printed brochure.

Visitors are usually seeking information. Design your site to make it easy to find.

Provide easy-to-understand language and design that clearly shows those categories of information most likely to be useful to the consumer. The user should not have to work to figure out how to find the basic information that describes your product or service.

Colonial Williamsburg offers an electronic brochure divided into categories—Dining,

Accommodations, What to See and Do, Shopping. Each section is designed to help the user plan the best experience at Colonial Williamsburg.

Easy, straightforward navigation is probably the single most important feature of an internet brochure. If users can't get to the information they need, they will get frustrated and go quickly to the competition. Remember, your competitors are just a click away.

Note: Users should not be required to download special programs to view streaming video to get basic information. It's fine to use these programs to create features that enhance the usefulness of the site, but there should be a version that all users can use without having to enhance their browser software in any way.

Use customization to sell.

Some marketers use their site to carry a static version of their print brochure in a PDF format, which saves documents electronically. The saved PDF opens in Adobe Acrobat and if you already have a print brochure, this is the most inexpensive way to put your brochure online. However, posting a static PDF does not make the most of the opportunity to respond and interact with your customers.

Interactivity can be a powerful selling tool.

At the Ford site, users can custom build and price their own vehicle. They can use a "Vehicle Advisor Tool" to better understand which particular kind of car might best fit their needs. They can apply for credit and "get a fast and easy credit decision" online without even going into a dealer. These customized modules take the site far beyond the printed brochure in providing real service.

Use the web site for promotions.

Web sites can be quickly updated at low cost. Use yours to advertise the latest specials.

> *JetBlue's web site is easy to use, short on gimmicks, and long on information and service. On any given day, the site has a myriad of special deals that make it feel fresh and alive.*

Hotels and car rental agencies now regularly reserve their best prices for those coming through the internet. This provides an incentive to "webify" the relationship between the company and the customers, thereby driving down transaction costs.

Your web site is an extension of your brand.

For many consumers, your internet brochure will be the principal way they learn about you. If it feels flat, if it's difficult to use, if it's never updated, the consumer will look elsewhere for information. If your information is stale or boring, competition will have a tremendous advantage.

Every web site should have a call-to-action.

Printed brochures cannot create the same kind of direct connections as their online counterpart. Use this to your advantage.

Transactions. The most direct result of a prospect coming to your site is to have them make a purchase. That can mean everything from purchasing theater tickets to booking a hotel room.

Lead generation. In instances where direct purchase is not practical, a lead can be generated for follow-up by a salesperson.

Questions and inquiries. For consumers not yet ready to buy, web sites provide mechanisms to ask questions or receive e-mail updates that might get them closer to the purchase decision. E-mail is an extension of the brochure.

Web sites and e-commerce

The ability to search, get information about products 24/7, see multiple images of those products, and purchase directly without speaking to a live operator—these are the things consumers say they like about online shopping.

On the other hand, millions of shoppers refuse to purchase online, mainly because they are afraid that their private credit card information will be stolen. Privacy concerns and identity theft are the biggest barriers to broader adoption of online purchase. Despite the fact that the risk of such fraud is not demonstrably higher online than it is when giving out credit card information over the phone or at retail, the psychological aspects of internet shopping mandate that catalog merchants view privacy and security as a primary marketing challenge.

Lands' End, one of the most successful online merchants, includes a "Security Statement" on its web site. The first sentence reads: "Since landsend.com went live in 1995, there has never been a confirmed case of fraud reported by our customers as a result of a credit card purchase made with us." This gives new users the confidence to shop at Lands' End.

Today, millions of consumers happily shop online, and internet catalogs have become an established form of selling. It's not surprising that some of the most profitable players are those who previously mastered the art of offline catalog sales—companies like Wal-Mart and L.L. Bean. They understand that the web is just another distribution channel that allows consumers to take advantage of their backend infrastructure investment.

Still, most successful players, large and small, approach the web differently than they do the printed catalog. One of our principal themes in this book is that the internet is a *different medium*, and must be approached differently. It is important that your brand "speak" to the online audience in the language of that medium.

With easily available transaction processing software now accessible by almost any size organization, the smallest merchants are selling their wares online. Major portals like Yahoo! provide turnkey services, design templates, and distribution for merchants and then take a slice of the revenue pie. Go to Yahoo! and search for fudge and you'll find choices from Godiva to the Alaskan Fudge Company. You'll even find soy fudge from the Value Nutrition Center.

There are a few relatively simple things to keep in mind when designing an online catalog:

1. **Put the consumer in the center of your design.** Internet shoppers are the same people who wander into stores and use print catalogs. Research shows that those most likely to shop online are *already* heavy users of offline catalogs, so your offline customers are the likeliest candidates for your online brand.

Your online shoppers want to find the products they're looking for. A prominent search box will make it easy for them to type in "shoes" if that's what they want. But not everyone uses a search box. So a well-designed catalog will also navigate users to the products they want from easily understood categories.

The Gap categorizes all of its merchandise into six main areas—Women, Men, Maternity, GapBody, Gap Kids, and Baby Gap. This simple site architecture helps consumers quickly find the merchandise they're looking for.

2. Impulse purchase is as powerful online as off. Most consumer purchases, from the supermarket to the bookstore, are unplanned. The merchandiser's art is to place products in such a way as to sell people things they don't even know they want. The same holds true online.

> *Wal-Mart has a huge online catalog. Shoppers are invited to "Sign up for more values" by entering their e-mail address. Wal-Mart uses that to e-mail new ideas even when users are not on the* Wal-Mart.com *site.*
>
> *Savvy catalog marketers use point-of-sale to close more business. When you purchase from the Barnes & Noble site (*www.bn.com*), you'll always be presented at checkout with ideas that might fit your reading tastes.*

Even small web catalogs can benefit from impulse behavior. By featuring hot products and internet-only specials on your home page, you can entice people exactly the way retailers do with their storefronts.

3. Use the internet as an order entry mechanism. Your print users may want the convenience of using the catalog while they order online. While many of your print customers may eventually want to use a web version of your catalog, the benefits of print will be with us for a long time. It's portable. The photography is wonderful. It's easy to browse. And it's familiar.

But many people—particularly the vast number of internet users at work—might not want to talk to a live person. For that reason, consider creating a prominent position on your home page to allow users to enter the catalog order number quickly and easily. This will provide your print customers with a convenient way to buy, while providing you with an efficient new order entry vehicle.

 4. Take advantage of interactivity. One of the best and most successful internet catalogs is the one managed by Dell, the big computer company. Dell publishes printed catalogs that it distributes by mail and through freestanding inserts. But its online catalog really shines.

Dell has created an incredibly easy-to-use customization tool that allows users to choose the exact features they want—the amount of memory, the type of monitor, the customer support plan. Configuring a personal computer transforms a world of confusion to a form of play.

In a completely different category, but using exactly the same principles, Lands' End has created an application called "My Model" that demonstrates how different color and style combinations might look on you. It turns the often painful guesswork of clothes shopping into a game.

But you needn't be a billion-dollar company to take advantage of interactivity. Beach Camera, an electronics store in New Jersey, has a comparison-shopping tool that shows users how to stack the features of one product against others. Creating useful and fun tools needn't be expensive and can help differentiate your catalog from the thousands of others online.

5. Consider a partnership with a major portal. It's one thing to create an online catalog—web design consultants are ubiquitous. It's quite another to get it noticed. Even very large players like Sony depend to some extent on portals for customer traffic. It's like having a good retail location in a mall. You go where the customers are.

As a small player, it's virtually impossible to get noticed on the vast sea of the internet. One way to increase your chances is to sign up with a portal like Yahoo! By becoming a part of their shopping service, you can raise the chances that customers will find you when they search for a specific product. Millions of customers have already come to trust Yahoo! with their credit card numbers.

The downside, of course, is that Yahoo! controls the customer, has access to the customer information, and takes a part of the transaction. That's the price you pay for their enormous customer base. And this will be true of all the large shopping portals.

There is no question that the internet is here to stay as a catalog medium. Will it replace print catalogs? Not likely anytime soon. In fact, retailers like Amazon and Red Envelope—who were born online—have gone on to produce printed catalogs as well. But as an additional, powerful way to reach millions of customers, the internet is a wonderful way to achieve global reach.

SUCCESSFUL CATALOGS

Unlike a brochure, a catalog provides everything needed to close a transaction—product options, prices, and order information.

Although shopping on the internet is increasing, many e-mail shoppers still prefer to browse through a printed catalog first. The most profitable retail mix combines stores, catalogs, and the internet.

Eddie Bauer has 570 stores, mails 110 million catalogs every year, and offers five web sites. Shoppers who use all three spend five times more than those who shop only by catalog. The higher the shoppers' income, the more likely they are to want several shopping methods.

Another route to profitability is to create upscale catalogs for high-end products.

For a holiday mailing, Disney created a larger catalog, printed on heavier stock, with more expensive products for children. The result was an increase in average order and units per order.

Bergdorf Goodman produced a holiday piece that used black-and-white photos shot and produced in four-color, which gave them unusual richness and depth.

Yet another trend in profitable catalogs is specialization. Lands' End produces a catalog just for plus-sized women; Talbot's creates one for petites as well. Whatever you are selling, these principles for more effective catalogs will help you sell more of it.

The cover is your showcase.

If you put a product on the cover, it will sell three times better than if it were placed on an inside page. The cover also sets the personality of the catalog—and the brand.

Sephora designed a striking cover for its holiday catalog of beauty products. It featured a model in gold-striped body paint and purple eye shadow—exactly the colors of Sephora's signature gift package.

Tip: If you put an item on the cover, it pays to give the page number where it can be found inside. Other traditional "hot spots"—places where merchandise tends to attract more notice—include the back cover, inside front and back covers, the center spread, the page next to the order form, and page one.

Make it easy for customers to order.

Organize your layout so readers can pair descriptions with photos. A bound-in order blank, while adding expense, may increase your sales. Think about testing to find out. If you include one, allow the customer ample space to write in necessary information, such as credit card number.

Think about the convenience of buyers who are using both a catalog and e-mail. Display your URL right alongside the toll-free telephone number. Always cross-reference codes in the catalog so prospects who want to buy online can simply type in a product ID.

Pack the copy with facts, not fantasy.

The trick, say professional catalog writers, is to *anticipate* the consumer's questions and answer them in the copy.

> "*The people who are going backpacking depend on our products for their comfort,*" *says a spokesman for Eddie Bauer.* "*They are vitally interested in details about buttons, zippers, wind-resistance. These customers read every word.*"

Keep an eye on your competition.

Are they ahead of you with innovative production techniques, like ink-jet messages on front or back cover? Are they controlling costs with lighter-weight paper, less expensive photography?

> *Women's clothing retailer Coldwater Creek uses no models. That not only saves money, it's become a symbol of the brand and its marketing philosophy that the customer wants to visualize herself in their clothes.*

Repeat your winners.

Always include those tried-and-true products that never fail to garner orders. Include a winner in a "bundle"—a group of items sold together at a reduced total cost.

 Give new items a good position so you can evaluate how well they do. Establish a level of performance and weed out merchandise that fails to meet it.

Mail to your list often.

The experts say it pays to mail four, five, six times a year—and more. Mail even more frequently to your best customers.

Test-mail your catalog more than once in the same season. Give it a fresh look by changing the cover.

Consider producing a smaller, less expensive mini-catalog to mail when you are prospecting for new customers.

From love poems to web sites

Pamphlets are the oldest advertising medium. They go back to the twelfth century, to a love poem in a little booklet. Over the centuries, brochures have wooed lovers, started wars, and changed ideas.

Brochures and catalogs may be small but they sell big-ticket items through the mail, even luxury cars or full-length fur coats. Their evolution into internet catalogs, as web sites, was a natural.

Not everyone has a budget for media advertising. Almost every business needs and produces sales pieces. You can use these marketing tools with other media. They can also stand on their own.

14 Promotion

The big word in promotion these days is "experiential." Advertisers have discovered that the more points of contact—and the greater the depth of connection—consumers have with a brand, the more loyal they are likely to be. Many promotions use all the leverage of a total marketing mix: television, print, radio, the internet, and, increasingly, some kind of hands-on interaction with the consumer.

- *At Atlanta's baseball stadium, Coke runs a dedicated "Coca-Cola Experience" section, where people come to mingle, dance, and, most of all, sip sodas.*
- *Lincoln, a sponsor of the U.S. Open, turned an unused building at the tennis center into the "Lincoln American Luxury Immersion," where visitors interacted with scenes of tennis throughout the ages and took a Lincoln on a "virtual" test drive. The result: 30,000 qualified leads.*
- *Budweiser has its Bud World, three 53-foot trailers that annually visit 120 markets across the country.*

- *GQ magazine made its temporary "GQ Lounge" a hot spot for Hollywood celebrities. "We wanted to find a creative new way for consumers to connect with our advertisers' products outside the pages of the magazine," says Daria Fabian, the magazine's head of marketing and promotion. There were several Cadillac Escalades parked outside and, inside, a chandelier made from 200 Bombay Sapphire gin bottles.*

For years, the ultimate promotion has been to reduce the price of products with coupons and rebates. Today, more advertisers recognize that short-term incentives do not take the place of a compelling long-term reason to buy.

Couponing continues to have its fans among consumers. According to a survey by *Brand Marketing* magazine, directed by Greenfield Online, 80 percent of Americans say they use coupons to stretch the family budget. No wonder they agree that the higher the face value, the better. Respondents say they use coupons most to buy their regular brand, so it's a loyalty program rather than an outreach.

Couponing is still very much with us today—in Sunday newspapers (FSIs), direct mail, on-pack coupons, and in-store circulars. The internet, growing quickly as a promotional medium, is the next frontier on the distribution front. Just remember that a coupon is a price cut (and lowers the value of a brand).

A coupon may be a good idea, but it's not a promotion.

BUILDING VALUE WITH PROMOTION

Here are some value-building promotion principles.

1. Promotions should be strategic. Too many promotions are created in a vacuum—"Let's run a sweepstakes" or "Let's sponsor a golf tournament." Start with brand objectives and a strategy and look for promotions that grow organically from a unified marketing plan.

Amazon.com offers customers free delivery on any orders over $25. This service not only supports Amazon's positioning as a low-cost merchant, but also is an incentive for shoppers to buy more merchandise.

2. Look for big ideas you can repeat year after year. Instead of running dozens of little promotions, advertisers have found it more effective to select just two or three big ones. Look for "anniversary" promotions that can be repeated at the same time every year.

- *Every year, Southern Comfort celebrates Mardi Gras in New Orleans, the city where the brand was born.*
- *Target Stores transformed a 220-foot-long glass-topped boat—painted with hundreds of red target logos—into a floating store, and anchored it at a Manhattan pier during the Christmas season.*
- *A pre-Christmas Toys Я Us Holiday Parade in Times Square—with music, entertainment, and personal appearances—paraded children's characters (and toys.)*

"You can't find big ideas unless you're looking for them, unless you need them, unless you insist upon them," says Jerry Welsh, the marketing whiz who created cause-related marketing—among other big ideas—for American Express. "You've got to believe that big ideas are not merely nice to have but are at the heart of success."

The cause-related marketing program at American Express started with local promotions supporting a community resource like a zoo. It then worked as a national promotion, for the restoration of the Statue of Liberty. It worked around the world. Today, cause-related marketing efforts are among the most successful—and best-publicized—promotions of all.

General Mills' Yoplait yogurt urges its consumers to "Save Lids to Save Lives." For every lid sent in, Yoplait donates ten cents to the Susan G. Komen Breast Cancer Foundation. In a recent year, more than five million lids meant more than one million dollars to the foundation, while Yoplait's volume rose 20 percent.

3. Pretest promotions. Pretesting need not be expensive. For packaged goods, you can use small samples of target households, or just a few stores for readable in-store tests. Split-store panels can be quickly checked with UPC scanning systems.

If you offer a coupon, test the face value and the way it is delivered—by mail, in a newspaper or magazine, on-pack or other means.

Before you decide on a premium, make sure of its appeal. Consumers often say one thing, but do another. They may tell you that they want a pocket thesaurus, when they actually prefer the steak knives. Internet testing, with real offers, can help you decide.

For services and nonpackaged goods products, where scanning data is not available, you can test via direct mail, the internet, or on-site audits.

4. Track the results. Keep records of promotions and how they've worked. Look for trends and patterns, and establish principles that guide future programs. Capture knowledge over time. Many otherwise astute advertisers fall down on this guideline.

5. Keep it simple. "If the idea comes with four pages of rules," says promotion expert Pierce Pelouze, former head of promotion at Campbell Soup Company, "turn it down." He adds that the idea must be easily grasped by the least educated, least experienced person who will come in contact with the promotion. This applies to consumers, the trade, and your own salespeople.

6. Advertise trial-builders. If you're running a promotion designed to build loyalty among current users, such as an in-package coupon, advertising directed at a broad audience is wasted. But a promotion aimed at encouraging trial among new users is usually worth supporting with some kind of marketing effort. The rule of thumb—add advertising only when you need to achieve a measurable increment over what the promotion could achieve on its own.

To attract new clients, H&R Block, the tax company, advertised a million-dollar sweepstakes: "Come in for your taxes. Come out a millionaire." Print, TV, radio, online, and direct mail all helped to spread the word that every customer using a Block retail office to handle returns was automatically entered. New client business was up 7 percent during the two-month promotional period.

7. Build campaigns. A key contribution of promotion is that it brings the advertising to life via special events such as lifestyle programs or sampling in malls. These orchestrated events can all contribute to the brand image.

Nobody does strategic promotion better than Jack Daniel's, which ties its promotions to the heritage established by Mr. Jack, who first began to blend his famous whiskey in the little town of Lynchburg,

Tennessee, back in 1850. "Mr. Jack's Birthday" is celebrated in countries all over the world almost every September, as lovers of Jack Daniel's gather at bars, pubs, boîtes, and teahouses to hoist a few in his honor.

A web site takes visitors on a virtual tour of the brewery. Some fans of Jack Daniel's want to visit Lynchburg, and the Visitor's Center offers guided tours of the brewery and the town (pop. 360).

8. Involve the trade. Think about customized promotions that will benefit the trade, as well as the consumer. More and more account-specific promotions are being run today.

Hormel has run its successful Hams for the Holidays promotion for over a dozen years. Retailers win points for the number of cases they sell. The points translate into the number of Hormel hams the retailer receives to donate to local charities.

9. Build relationships. Stay in touch with the lifestyles of your target audience, and customize your promotions to suit their often changing needs.

After a year of consumer research, Guinness changed its entire promotional mix. Instead of sponsoring a more traditional Irish concert, for example, it recognized the preferences of its young male audience by sponsoring Lit, Papa Roach, and Big Head Todd.

10. Stretch your dollars with the right partnerships. Look for partners who market to the same target audience, and whose "brand essence" is similar to yours. Brand synergies add impact to joint promotion.

Bally, the chain of health clubs, deals with a number of partners, including Kraft Foods, Pepsi, Kellogg's, Kodak, and Dove toilet bar. Bally partners value the on-pack offers of over $25 for special memberships in the club—made on products that sell for less than $4. Retail stores in most of the fitness centers make Bally a good distribution partner as well.

Sampling also works. Health clubs provide one of the most popular venues for reaching affluent young people, together with movie theaters, offices of doctors, dentists, and veterinarians, college dormitories, and sports stadiums.

DISPLAYS

As retailers focus on motivating existing customers to spend more, displays—especially customized displays that match various shopper profiles—are increasingly important.

"Storyboard the store," urges promotion expert Mel Korn. "From the moment the shopper enters the store, nothing should be left to chance." Korn believes that every aisle should provide clues to other aisles and other categories where shoppers can find solutions to their needs. This added creativity makes the shopping experience more rewarding for the consumer, and can increase sales for the retailer as well.

But a display works only if it is displayed. There are two targets for effective in-store material.

- *It must be something that the retailer wants to display.*
- *It must be a compelling story to the consumer.*

This is a reversal of the historic priority of designing displays (and promotions) primarily for consumers. It recognizes the shift in power to the large retailer. Wal-Mart, for example, attracts millions of shoppers every day! But getting on the shelf—and on display—is another matter.

Store managers like appealing point-of-purchase (POP) displays. They help move merchandise and make stores more exciting. They must also conform to the store image and its display policies.

A good display can increase the level of trade support, move the brand on its merits (without price-cutting), sell anywhere in the store (checkouts, for example), organize and accommodate your entire line, and provide strong brand identification. Scanners now provide us with proof that good displays produce sales.

Some display principles to think about.

Involve the trade.

Include something the retailer needs or wants—a board to display prices, a clock, or some premium to take home.

Swiss Army knives were "dead" merchandise, hidden under store counters until someone asked for one. Retailers were persuaded to buy a countertop display filled with knives, with the promise they could return it if it didn't become the highest margin square foot in the store. This promotion created an impulse business that grew from $2 million to $20 million. Not one display was returned.

Involve your customer.

When you can involve customers at the point of purchase, you bring them closer to the sale. Encourage consumers to pick up a product, taste it, or try it.

Estée Lauder helped introduce its Spotlight skin tone perfector with a display that invited potential customers to test the product themselves.

Think local.

Tailor the display (and even the product) to the neighborhood and the store.

Part of Wal-Mart's successful strategy is to offer products that fit the needs of shoppers in local markets. The retailer asked Hormel to come up with a line of snack foods it could display in those stores that had important hunting and fishing aisles. Hormel came up with "Spamouflage"—Spam in camouflage cans. Within weeks, Wal-Mart gave the brand special display space in 760 of its rural stores.

Make the display easy to set up.

And easy to take care of.

Club Med's display, designed to hold brochures, resembles a lifeguard station, complete with beach umbrella on top. It is die-cut and shipped flat, with a minimum of assembly. The retailer needs only to replace the brochures as they are depleted or new ones are produced.

Tie in to your advertising.

Use key visuals to present a unified image.

Remember seasons and holidays.

Good reasons for a store manager to *want* to put up your display.

Use new technology for flexibility and cross-selling.

New technology, like electronic labels that receive instructions from a radio transmitter, allows price tags to be changed at a moment's notice. These products not only save on manpower, but give the store manager flexibility to offer time-dependent specials. If the tomatoes are reaching their peak and need to be moved, the store can make a quick price cut in the evening. If there is a sudden downpour, it might change the price on umbrellas.

A scanner known as SAM (Shoppers Answer Machine) gives product information and cross-sells. For example, if a shopper in aisle 2 scans a flashlight, the monitor can display information that there is a special sale on batteries in aisle 5.

The product—not the display—is the hero.

If possible, locate the display apart from the usual product location. Try to make it compatible with another category—a wine display in the cheese section, a pretzel display in the beer aisle.

Promotions in stores can do something not possible in any other medium—they can let people experience the product. The opportunity to let consumers see, feel, smell, or taste products has long been well understood by retailers; now advertisers are recognizing its importance. In-store sampling or customized promotions with retailers allow products to come out of their packages. Don't underestimate the power of sensory appeals to get people to try your product.

The new point of sale

One of the interesting developments in promotion is an internet arrangement called "the virtual end-cap." In travel, the traditional point of sale was the travel agent. Now more people are researching their trips online, so airlines and car rental agencies are placing their promotions at the new point of sale—the online booking agent—to influence purchase.

When you book a trip on Travelocity, U.S. Airways hits you with a full-page "interstitial" (an advertising unit that appears between one page and another) promoting their flight to the destination you've selected.

EVENT MARKETING

Sports and musical events are far and away the most popular sponsorships, but there are thousands of other events that can match the brand with its target audience.

Recognize first that event marketing is not necessarily efficient. Sponsorship is just the beginning—you may want to advertise it, merchandise it, and involve the trade. Be prepared to spend two to three times the amount you would on advertising alone.

Fleetwood Homes not only sponsored country singer Neal McCoy's tour, it invited audiences at each concert to enter a contest to win a free home. Concertgoers were sent to retail locations to see if they had won, and those who toured homes received a McCoy CD. Consumer advertising consisted of television and print, while a direct-mail campaign kept retailers informed. Calls to Fleetwood's hotline tripled and 25 percent more retailers joined the program.

CONTESTS AND SWEEPSTAKES

As these proliferate, especially on the internet, the grand prizes become more expensive and more fantastic. Winners have been sent to Bora Bora to swim with sharks, to remote deserts to excavate dinosaur bones, to explore the wreckage of the *Titanic* in a submersible, and to ride the world's most terrifying roller coasters. Other popular prizes are walk-on roles in television programs or Hollywood films. The key remains finding a theme relevant to the brand.

Food Network conducted an on-air sweepstakes in which one high school won celebrity chef Emeril Lagasse for a day as cafeteria cook. As first prize in another contest, the network sent the winner and three friends on a gourmet trip via private jet.

PRODUCT PUBLICITY

The art of product publicity is to get a third party—the media—to talk about your product in a favorable manner. Third-party endorsements by columnists, authors, editors, reporters, and TV news personalities carry a clout that paid advertising cannot.

Get your story to lifestyle editors, broadcast-news assignment editors, talk-show producers, and trade publications. Give them a "hook" that makes it newsy.

To drive trial and awareness for its Max Life Motor Oil, Valvoline launched a search for a consumer willing to live in his car while driving cross-country. The winner went on a 52-day tour of retail outlets, and was interviewed by more than 40 media sources along the way. Revenues for Max Life rose 160 percent.

Sometimes it's necessary to build the appropriate promotion values into the product. Not many people were eating "horse mackerel" salads or sandwiches until a persuasive PR man renamed the product "tuna fish."

Harold Burson, a dean of the PR business, believes in advertising *with* publicity. In his words:

First, it enhances the credibility of the advertising message. The publicity must be timed to appear first; then when people see the ads, they pay attention. "It also extends the message. There is a tyranny in the 30-second commercial that a news story can overcome, by providing more information.

Think Headlines and Messages

What is the headline you would like to see for your product or service? What are the messages you want delivered?

News releases are not the game, and are unlikely on their own to produce the desired headlines or stories. There are several tactics that command attention.

- *Press conferences for news that won't wait*
- *Video news releases or satellite feeds*
- *Media tours*

The best way to place a good story is the less dramatic but effective one-on-one tailored presentation, with a journalist with whom you have built a long-term relationship of candor and respect.

Publicity people must have a nose for news. They must consider every news story for what it could mean to a client's product or service, then pitch that story to the media.

Creating a Communications Program

Start with the assumption that a publicity program is accountable, and the way to measure its success is not with stacks of press clippings.

Set actionable objectives. Segment the public—the media and *their* audiences—and get agreement on the messages for each audience. *Measure the results.* Concentrate on quality and results against the objectives. Talk to the sales force, make sure your press release has an 800 number and a URL, and conduct attitudinal surveys.

Publicity is not about answering questions from the media. It is about getting the media to buy a strategic message—your story.

15 Truth and Ethics

There are things we do in advertising because they are the law, and things we do because they are right.

What is *truthful* is clearly determined by the law.

What is *right* is a matter of corporate conscience—an extralegal responsibility to be taken just as seriously as legal ones.

The erosion of public confidence in institutions and public figures can only make consumers more suspect of advertising, which has long been questioned as to its veracity and responsibility. There will always be misleading advertising that manages to slip through the legal and regulatory screens. Yet people are surprised to learn of the essential truthfulness of advertising and the policies that keep it that way. They are amazed when told, for example, that consumer testimonials must reflect what is true—not just what people think or are willing to say on camera (for money).

Perhaps the real surprise is that, with the continuing exposure of fresh scandals in the business world, advertising has managed to police itself and be policed to become a responsible marketing force.

Much of the federal legislation that regulates advertising started when the Federal Trade Commission was created by Congress in 1914 to deal with "deceptive and unfair acts and practices in commerce."

The FTC isn't the only agency that polices advertising, and that isn't all they do. They have Telemarketing Sales Rules (including a proposed new rule to create a one-stop "do not call" list), and continue to monitor "spam."

More than 30 statutes allow others to scrutinize advertising, including:

- *The Food and Drug Administration for foods, drugs, and cosmetics.*
- *The United States Postal Service for mailed advertising materials.*
- *The Federal Communications Commission for radio and television advertising.*
- *The Securities and Exchange Commission for stock and bond advertising.*
- *The Electronic Communications Privacy Act protecting personal data on the internet.*
- *The Children's Online Privacy Protection Act (COPPA) placing parents in control of what information is collected from their children online. The FTC has enabled members of online marketing and telemarketing industry groups to provide "safe harbors" by creating self-regulatory rules—which must be approved by the FTC.*

States get into the act as well. The National Association of Attorneys General has become increasingly active.

Ignorance of the law is no excuse, as we have learned. There are clear legal principles for advertising, and it pays to know them.

1. Tell the truth, show the truth. If the dessert melts under the hot camera lights, too bad. You can't tamper with it or make it firmer. If the dog won't eat the dog food, that's your problem. Under no conditions can you doctor it with bacon to get the dog to eat. Campbell Soup and its agency paid a price for adding marbles to the soup so viewers could see the vegetables.

Your product must be shown exactly as the consumer buys it—in all *material* respects.

You cannot have a product specially selected or constructed for use in advertising. Take it right off the production line. This is particularly true of product demonstrations.

> *Advertising showed a giant-tired truck flattening every car in a row but the Volvo. It was later found that the Volvo's roof had been reinforced and supports of the other cars weakened.*
>
> *Although the Volvo was strong enough to hold the truck's weight, this was seen as a misrepresentation of a material fact. The Federal Trade Commission fined both the advertiser and agency.*

Packages can be cleaned up to be more legible in advertising. Things that don't impinge on product performance can be touched up. But the product is inviolate.

Glasses in a beer advertisement cannot be retouched to make the beer appear lighter or darker. A blemish on the beer drinker's cheek—not material to the sale of the product—can be retouched. A blemish on a woman's cheek in a skin care advertisement, however, is material and cannot be altered.

Avoid strange camera angles or unusual props that make the product look other than it is, such as a smaller-than-normal cereal bowl to make a portion look larger.

2. Make the general impression truthful. Advertising is judged not by what it says, but by what the consumer *thinks* it says.

> *A food product together with an eight-ounce glass of milk is a nutritionally balanced meal. If the consumer thinks the product is complete by itself—even if the milk is mentioned or shown—the advertising is deceptive.*

If research indicates consumers are getting the wrong impression, correct it. Otherwise the FTC can rule that the advertising is deliberately intended to deceive.

Disclaimers need not be dull.

> *A commercial for a Roy Rogers promotion depicts a concerned father asking his prospective son-in-law how the couple plans to eat. On learning the answer, "Bacon cheeseburgers from Roy's," the father remarks, "Surely, you don't plan to eat bacon cheeseburgers the rest of your life?" "Relax. No sweat," the young man replies. "It's a limited-time offer."*

3. Ban "weasels" and dangling comparisons. "This printer can give you the fastest copies you've ever seen." The weasel is "can," which the consumer is likely to miss.

"This printer will give you faster copies." That's a dangling comparison. Faster than what? Faster than the printer used to, or faster than the competition? Make it clear.

4. Substantiate product claims. There are subjective claims about a product that cannot be substantiated—beautiful hair color, a smooth ride, "fried chicken like Mother used to make."

Then there are objective or competitive claims—longer lasting than other hair colorings, a smoother ride than any full-size sedan. For these, you must have high-quality research or evidence the claim is true, and you must be able to prove that a majority of consumers agree.

5. Back testimonials with research. Several consumers may be convinced that your product does things better than anything on the market and may be willing to say so on television. That's not enough.

- *You need evidence that the product will in fact do what the people say it will do.*
- *These people must represent a majority of consumers, not an aberrational few.*
- *They must have come to these views before "consideration" (money) was involved or before they knew there was a possibility of being paid.*

If celebrities are identified as using a product, they must have been using it before being approached (and be able to prove it) and must continue to use it as long as the campaign runs.

Who Is Responsible?

The advertiser and the agency are separately and equally responsible for advertising presented to the consumer. *Separately* and *equally*.

The advertiser cannot take on the entire responsibility and absolve the agency of liability.

Each is considered especially knowledgeable in areas of its own expertise. The advertiser is responsible for providing accurate product information, which the agency (without its own technical research facility) can accept. The agency, on its part, is responsible for truthful photography of the product, accurate documentation of demonstrations, and substantiation of testimonials.

Both agency and advertiser should be represented at preproduction meetings and on the set when a question might arise. Don't take anything for granted.

ADVERTISING AND RESPONSIBILITY

The first responsibility is to protect the consumer, by telling people what they need to know in order to make an informed choice.

Information about products and services, with some sensible limits, is clearly in the public interest—ingredient disclosures on proprietary medicines and nutritional information on food products, for example. The place to start is on the package itself, with clear and informative labeling.

Responsibility draws us into new areas like privacy and telemarketing as well as longstanding concerns about tobacco, advertising to children, and political advertising.

Privacy

The use of what people consider private information is of growing concern to consumer advocates, legislators, and the media. The growth of the internet has added to this concern and pressure for legislation.

A pharmaceutical company agreed to settle federal charges that it violated its own privacy policies when it inadvertently released the e-mail addresses of hundreds of people taking one of their products.

The company was required to improve its online security, including better training for employees. The Federal Trade Commission had charged that the company's privacy policies were deceptive because the company failed to back them up with the appropriate security.

The key quote from the FTC's director of consumer protection:

Even the unintentional release of sensitive medical information is a serious breach of consumer's trust. Companies that obtain sensitive information in exchange for a promise to keep it confidential must take appropriate steps to ensure the security of that information.

The privacy debate grows with the ever-increasing availability of consumer data and the ability to manage information. Detailed user profiles are being created by tracking web sites visited, advertisements viewed, and purchases made—gathered through internet technologies such as "cookies" and, more recently, "web bugs." The issue is whether people are being informed and consent to the use of their names for certain purposes.

The general rule is that you cannot ask for information about an individual. You can ask for lists of people who have similar characteristics in common—gender, income, type of residence, or buying habits.

"Databases of people's spending habits," observes *The New York Times*, "are simply too attractive a marketing tool." Many products and services would not exist without the free flow of personal consumer data. Where do we draw the line between these needs and the need to protect consumer privacy?

American Express collects information to enroll customers, to provide the services they have selected, to administer their accounts, and to offer them additional or related products or services. It also obtains information from other companies and public sources to identify customers who might be interested in specific products or services.

The company strongly advocates the protection of product information, and has long operated with published Privacy Principles:

1. *We collect only customer information that is needed, and we tell customers how we use it.*
2. *We give customers choices about how their data will be used.*
3. *We insure information quality.*
4. *We use information security safeguards.*
5. *We limit the release of customer information.*
6. *We are responsive to customers' requests for explanations.*
7. *We extend these privacy principles to our business relationships.*
8. *We hold employees responsible for our privacy principles.*

The policy puts teeth in the last point.

Employees who violate these Principles or other company policies and practices are subject to disciplinary action, up to and including dismissal. Employees are expected to report violations—and may do so confidentially—to their managers, to their business unit's compliance officer, or to the Office of the Ombudsperson.

Marketers must accept the principle of "informed consent." Consumers must know what information about them is on file and how it may be used, so they know they have the right to "opt out."

Raise your consciousness on this issue.

Telemarketing

You don't like being interrupted at dinner by a sales pitch? Really?

As telemarketing and other forms of advertising by telecommunications mushroomed in the '90s, a variety of federal and state statutes were adopted, aimed at regulating the use and misuse of these media.

Congress and more than 40 states limit the use of automatic dialing-announcement devices (ADADs) capable of making up to 1,500 telephone calls per day without an operator.

The U.S. Federal Trade Commission plans to create a national "Do not call" registry, making it illegal for telemarketers to call anyone on that list.

Tobacco

This product category is under intense regulation throughout the world. Tobacco cannot be advertised on broadcast media in the U.S., and print is heavily regulated as well.

There are other product categories, like prescription drugs and alcoholic beverages, that have legal requirements on how and where they can be advertised. Check the rules of your product category and make sure your advertising complies.

Advertising to Children

"Parents must educate children to become responsible and informed consumers," says the American Academy of Pediatrics.

As more and more parents spend more time producing income and less time tending their children, the burden of responsibility falls increasingly on the advertiser.

There have always been those who worry about media influences on children, from comic books to movies. Now there is increasing pressure to restrict or regulate advertising to children, both in the U.S. and in Europe. Some critics claim young children are too naïve to distinguish between advertising and programming. Others feel food marketing contributes to childhood obesity. Marketing in schools is a new concern, with cable networks offering free TVs with news programs—and commercials.

Advertisers claim that bans would lead to worse programming on television, fewer educational resources in schools, and higher prices for toys.

Both sides are missing the point, claims *The Economist*—". . . parents and teachers have a responsibility to teach children about the realities of a commercial world, just as they teach them how to cross a road safely."

Nevertheless, children are a special audience, and TV is a pervasive medium among those under ten. It is important not to distort a product's appearance or performance, not to suggest making friends is a reason to use a product, and not to encourage eating habits that could interfere with good nutrition.

Advertising to children can be effective and must be socially responsible.

Marketing to Children online

The old cliché that most parents learn to use computers and the internet from their kids was born of the idea that today's kids are as comfortable online as the baby boomers were with television. It's their medium. From downloading music to editing their own movies, kids seem to have a facility with interactive formats, and they take for granted the incredible resources that digital technologies provide.

Guidelines from the FTC and the Children's Advertising Review Unit (CARU, *www.caru.org*) call for clear separation of programming from advertising, a requirement that is becoming increasingly difficult in an internet world. Kids are online and marketers know that—just as they know that television is a place to find kids.

But there is a huge difference between these two media. As a two-way medium, the web can be abused in ways that are simply impossible on television. Unscrupulous marketers can find ways to collect personal information from children, including their name and address, which in the wrong hands can have devastating effect, from fraud to pedophilia.

That's why the Federal Trade Commission developed COPPA—the Children's Online Privacy Protection Act (*www.ftc.gov/ogc/coppa1.htm*), which went into effect in April 2000. Among other things, the law now stipulates that web sites must get permission from parents before collecting, using, or disclosing personal information from children under 13.

Political Advertising

There are few more emotionally charged subjects than this one. Some groups want to ban it entirely, others point to fundamental First Amendment issues. As currently practiced, with so many negative messages and often so little credibility, it casts all advertising in a bad light.

Government officials must use contemporary media to communicate and lead, as well as to get elected, and ora-

tions are no longer the way to reach a mass audience.
Since we're stuck with some form of political advertising, it is reasonable to insist that it be both fair and true. There is a fine line between regulation and censorship of free speech, but it is around this issue that the debate should be engaged. Unlike product advertising, where the consumer just doesn't buy again if dissatisfied, political advertising leaves voters with a choice that affects their lives over the longer term.

Advertising Review Boards

It is tempting for marketing people to get swept up in their enthusiasm and miss some of their responsibilities. That's why some companies have set up advertising review boards to make sure they live up to the highest standards of law and responsibility.

The purpose of these boards is to ensure that all marketing and communications programs are truthful, clear, and in good taste, and to guard against consumer misrepresentation. They also act as an internal audit to substantiate advertising claims.

It is particularly important to set up standards for media, such as which television programs or magazines meet corporate standards. Special-interest pressure groups are prone to use threats of boycotts to influence media selections—to ban magazines like *Playboy* or *Hustler* or programs like *Sex in the City*—to meet their personal standards.

It's one thing for a company to decide it doesn't want to use these magazines or programs, but that's the company's decision to make. Without standards established in advance, advertisers can be whipsawed to follow someone else's standards.

One of the great contributions of the advertising community is the use of its talents to support community or social causes. Agencies donate their time and talent, various media donate time or space, TV and print production companies donate their capabilities, clients pay for out-of-pocket costs for production (usually without any markup).

Most public service announcements (PSAs) have been channeled through the Advertising Council, an association of advertisers, agencies, and media that takes on such causes as fighting drunk driving, community crime, and pollution.

A campaign to increase public involvement in championing art education in schools started with the headline: "No wonder people think Louis Armstrong [shown with his trumpet] was the first man to walk on the moon."

The ad concludes, "The less art kids get, the more it shows."

Some of the Ad Council's other current concerns are:

Domestic violence—"End Abuse. Teach early."

Colon Cancer Detection and Prevention—"Get the test. Get the polyp. Get the cure."

The September 11 attack on the World Trade Center led to advertising to raise funds for the families of victims, firemen, and policemen lost in that tragedy, plus a campaign to encourage visitors to return to New York City.

The New York campaign launched with Mayor Rudy Giuliani setting up the theme "Experience the New York Dream!"

The following commercials showed celebrities "experiencing" their New York Dream—Woody Allen figure skating at Rockefeller Center, Yogi Berra conducting the New York Philharmonic, Barbara Walters auditioning for a singing role, Henry Kissinger sliding into home plate at Yankee Stadium, Billy Crystal and Robert DeNiro riding a float in Macy's Thanksgiving Day Parade.

To make a difference, public service advertising must be just as disciplined and professional as commercial advertising. Broadcasters and publishers are bombarded by organizations asking for free time and space. The Ad Council alone sponsors 39 programs, and there are many other national and local individual efforts.

Getting public service advertising on air or in print is a huge challenge. Agencies love to create commercials or print ads that touch emotions for good causes. Boards of directors cheer. Then the advertising appears a few times in odd hours. Lots of time and money expended, with no lasting impact. Since the media can't run everything, they will choose advertising they want to run.

The commercial starts with blind musician Stevie Wonder playing the harmonica and saying "I can't say no." Other celebrities follow, citing frivolous things they can not *do—Harrison Ford ("I can't do math").*

It closes with Christopher Reeve in his wheelchair: "It doesn't matter who you are, there are things you can't do and things you can. It's about ability, *not disability." Then the logo of The National Organization on Disability (N.O.D.).*

 Specialist placement agency WestGlen offers these tips for a successful PSA.

- *The message must serve the public—but make the subject matter interesting.*
- *Make sure the message is relevant to the station or viewing area—localize spots whenever possible.*
- *Provide multiple commercial lengths—and send each station its preferred length. The most acceptable is :30, followed by :60 and :15.*

Radio PSAs can zero in on specific demographics, and spots can be localized for specific markets by recording local tags or providing local information for live delivery.

It's easier to get cleared on radio, says WestGlen, but TV offers more staying power. Radio moves spots in and out quickly, on average one to three months. A spot on TV can run on average three months, with many stations keeping it on for six months or longer.

What Is the Reader or Viewer Being Asked to Do?

There should always be some call to action—vote, put out campfires, contribute time or money—and a web site to browse or 800 number to call. The N.O.D. commercial asked viewers to visit its web site at *www.nod.org*.

What Are the Objectives and Strategy?

For public service or any other advertising, the most effective campaigns have one message and one image that they stay with year after year after year.

The Partnership for a Drug-Free America was set up to take on a single large social problem with a series of campaigns on the many faces of drug abuse. Recent commercials used Olympic athletes like 19-year-old U.S. Gold Medalist Apolo Ohno.

Am I a speed skater? Yes. Did I skate my way to a World Cup victory? Yes. Could I have skated this far if I'd ever done drugs? Pleassse.

How Will It Be Measured?

It's hard to get accurate numbers of how many times the advertising ran or how many people saw it. An Advertising Council Study with the Advertising Research Foundation found that TV commercials persuaded double the number of men to get screening tests for colon cancer, which increased the survival rate from 50 to over 90 percent. But few public service campaigns run long enough to make other than a short-term difference.

The reality is that a lot of public service announcements are run without much evidence of their effectiveness. They run on faith, for the benefit of good causes.

REGULATION AND RESPONSIBILITY

Advertising is a powerful medium. It comes into our homes and our lives, it reflects values, and it attracts attention. While its purpose is to sell, it must also have a sense of social responsibility. It can have a corrosive effect on social values if not handled carefully. Advertising does not exist in a vacuum nor can it be amoral.

For all these reasons, advertising is a highly visible target. Its excesses of bad taste (use of sexuality, questionable stereotypes, loud appeals) have been criticized, often with justification. Threats of regulation often follow criticism.

Advertising must be regulated by someone, and that someone is the advertising business, which must regulate itself—following the letter and the spirit of the law. Advertisers need to be responsible in advertising and product labeling. Agencies must insist that clients substantiate product claims. Broadcasters, publishers, and educators should be part of the process.

At stake are free speech and information and the right of consumers to choose rather than having choices made for them. Tell the truth, the whole truth, and nothing but the truth. And, remember, brands are built on trust.

16 Working With An Agency

"I believe in advertising," said John Pepper, former CEO of Procter & Gamble, "simply because I have seen throughout 25 years that the correlation between profitable—let me emphasize profitable—business growth on our brands and having great copy isn't 25 percent, it's not 50 percent, it's not 75 percent; it is 100 percent."

When advertising goes wrong or business softens, it's tempting to point at the agency.

"Maybe we should get a new agency."

Remember, *somebody* approved that advertising. Agencies don't do things alone. There is a reason why one client gets outstanding advertising from an agency, and another in the same agency gets something less. For advertising to go right, an agency needs the partnership of a strong client.

There must also be a *process* that allows ideas to get through the organization without being compromised or diluted. Creativity in advertising is like a triangle—the right agency, the right client, and the right process. Process is important. Someone must be in charge—an agency cannot take direction from a committee. Watch out for too many layers of approvals—they filter the vitality out of ideas. Beware of all those "little changes" that add up.

Even with the stars lined up perfectly, great advertising is still not guaranteed. Remove any one of these parts, and the odds of success are that much lower. Yet the first reaction when things go wrong is often to look for a new agency.

Agencies are generally hired on the basis of their creative abilities—the promise that they can create campaigns that will build a client's business. They are seldom fired for bad advertising alone, although that does happen.

The underlying reason for most agency changes is that the relationship has broken down. Advertisers don't want to be seen as bad guys by telling the truth—that they have lost trust in the agency's ability to deliver—so they say something soft to the press like "The business has changed" or "We need a fresh approach."

Perhaps the largest problem is communications.

> *Over the past decade, we have interviewed hundreds of client executives on behalf of advertising agencies. In every client satisfaction survey, the number one complaint from advertisers is 'communication.' There is never enough between advertiser and agency or, from the client's point of view, among agency departments.*
>
> —TONI MALONEY, THE MALONEY GROUP

The two biggest—and ongoing—gripes clients have about agencies are "Why does it take so long?" and "Why does it cost so much?" It takes so long because agencies have other fish to fry, and clients don't always realize this. They like to think their agency is solely focused on them. It costs so much for a multitude of reasons, chiefly miscommunications that fail to clearly state the problem to be solved. The solution—ground rules for consistent and effective communications.

Like all businesses, advertising goes through highs and lows. People on both sides must have confidence and trust in each other to work through the low points. Trust is often lost when there's a change in the relationship—someone new on either side. If that occurs when advertising is weak, there is no established relationship to pull it through.

Changing agencies is a pain in the neck, time-consuming, expensive, and not productive. It does nothing to move the business ahead. Far better to get the right agency from the start, learn to be a better client, and work on the relationship.

CREATE AN ENVIRONMENT FOR IDEAS

To be a better client, start by asking for big ideas. Set high standards—challenging questions get large answers. Let the agency know you are confident that they will deliver more than good, solid advertising—and that you expect more.

Remember you're dealing with a creative product. There is no formula for brilliance. Managing ideas requires a special sensitivity. There is a useful German expression, *fingerspitzen*—literally a feeling in the fingertips. Not everyone has this sensitivity, but it can be developed.

Insist on professional discipline. Clear strategies. Thoughtful creative briefs. Set objectives and stick with them. Tell people where you want to go, and be consistent.

Learn the fine art of conducting a creative meeting. Don't nitpick. Deal with the important issues first—strategy, consumer benefit, brand positioning, personality. State clearly whether the advertisement succeeds in these areas. And if not, why not. It frustrates a creative team to push themselves hard to come up with a great campaign, only to have the client deal with details. It's okay to tell people they have missed the target. Just don't leave them there guessing.

Try to react like a person, not a corporation. Be human. When you like the advertising, let everyone know you like it. Be frank when you don't like it—just give people a reason why you're turning it down. (They may even agree.) Be willing to admit you aren't sure. You may need time to absorb what they've been thinking about for weeks. Don't let anyone press you by asking for an immediate approval after a presentation of new work.

Be clear. Agencies have selective hearing—they are waiting for you to approve the advertising. Unless you are firm in turning down an idea, it will pop up again.

Make the agency feel responsible. Tell them what you think is wrong—not how to fix it. The best clients are not meddlers. Agencies work harder if someone points out the problems, then lets them find the solution. If they expect someone will always tell them what to do, they won't try as hard.

Keep agency people involved in your business. Tell them what's happening, good and bad. That includes creative people—they want to know the latest market shares, too. Your success is ultimately theirs.

Take advantage of the natural competition within an agency, and get people fighting to work on your advertising. Few clients understand that within an agency, the best people get to work on the best accounts. Otherwise, the agency cannot hold them. They do their best work for the clients they like and respect. That does not mean easy clients. It pays to care about being a good client.

EVALUATING AN AGENCY

A great relationship with an agency is built over time. Like a marriage, you have to work at it. One of the most important ways to nurture the relationship is to tell people what you think of them—honestly and in writing. The advertiser initiates the process—smart agencies welcome and ask for evaluations.

Many issues will be discussed informally during the year. That is no substitute for a formal annual written review of successes and shortcomings, of projects and people.

Look forward, not just backward. Set up a short list of three to five major objectives—specific goals that if accomplished could make a material impact on your business. Focus on big issues—strategic contributions, staffing, results—not whether the media plan was delivered on time.

Keep evaluations simple. Otherwise, nobody will do them. Additional review sessions during the year can eliminate the small irritations that creep into a relationship.

Some agencies sponsor client satisfaction studies conducted by a third party. Clients sometimes mask the truth because they don't like delivering bad news. "Talking to a third party eliminates this. These studies can fix things before they become unsolvable if conducted regularly, every six months or so," says agency executive Graham Phillips. "They can also be used as a benchmark for agency compensation."

Be an equal opportunity client—ask the agency to tell you how you can make the relationship better. Evaluations work both ways. But the whole process is worthless unless the most senior people at agency and client meet face to face to discuss the evaluation and agree on its fairness and the objectives.

AGENCY COMPENSATION

It is the agency's job, not the advertiser's, to control its costs. The agency cannot control revenue, however, except in the way it prices its services and gets paid. Advertisers must be conscious that every time someone touches the agency, they're spending money.

There are several ways to pay an agency—negotiated commissions on billings, labor-based pay for the number of hours worked (plus a profit), performance-based incentive systems, plus combinations of these.

More advertisers today are moving to "labor-based compensation." This system defines the work to be done and assigns responsibilities to both parties. Compensation is structured by calculating the *percent* of agency salaries (plus overhead) to complete the work assigned. The rationale is that the agency benefits by being fairly paid for the amount of work it does, and the advertiser benefits by paying for the work instead of for the media that is bought.

Be sensitive in applying any system. What is an idea worth—and what does it cost? How long does it take to create an idea? Some ideas are worth more than others.

But how to set the fee?

How to deal with new media, like interactive? What about use of creative work in other countries?

Whatever the plan, it should embrace several principles.

1. Incentives to build the client's business. The first principle is for the agency to identify with the client's business—on whatever measure is chosen. It is true that lots of things beyond advertising go into sales success. It is equally true that product, pricing, distribution, and other factors beyond the agency's control contribute to failure, yet the agency still suffers with a sick brand.

Advertisers can set up specific goals that are important to their business and reward agencies for achieving these, with cash payments for success, larger fees, or commissions on higher budgets. Agencies cannot live on year-end incentives alone—they have to pay people and pay the landlord every month, so there must be some kind of base payment.

Everyone is still searching for the Holy Grail of Accountability. Technology is getting us closer to a return-on-investment analysis, with measured response rates and results, although there are too many factors involved to get to a pure ROI number.

2. Incentives to the agency to control its costs. Advertisers generally don't pay their agencies for controlling costs. The incentive to the agency is profitability, the by-product of cost control. Agencies have three principal costs—people, rent, and (to a lesser extent) technology. A well-run agency keeps its rent as low as possible, so as not to put pressure on salaries.

Since the largest cost by far is people, solving problems the first time around, rather than going back time and again, is the ultimate cost-saver.

3. A fair profit over time. A profitable agency does better work, and profitable accounts within an agency attract better people. Word gets around fast—people don't want to hitch their careers to marginal or unprofitable accounts.

A fair profit does not mean a guaranteed profit. Agencies expect to invest in learning a new business or in start-up situations or in tough times. They can't afford to invest year after year.

The major advertising associations can provide figures on industry averages for agencies or accounts of different sizes. A 20 percent pretax operating profit was a rule-of-thumb for many years, and some still realize that target. It can be a starting point for discussion.

Advertisers should be unwilling to subsidize average profits for below-average work, but pleased to pay a great deal more for success.

4. A plan that is simple to administer. You want to spend your time discussing advertising, not compensation. Be wary of complex systems that entail multiple meetings and lots of forms. Keep it simple.

Brendan Ryan, CEO of FCB and former chairman of the American Association of Advertising Agencies (4As), believes there is too little emphasis on effectiveness and accountability. He says people are losing faith in the most fundamental principles of the business: "Run good advertising. Sell more stuff. Build brands better. Make more profits."

CONSULTANTS

Do you need a new logo, package design, or web page? Want to reinvigorate your brand? There are consultants available for all these special needs—and more. There are marketing consultants, branding consultants, design consultants, media consultants, web design consultants, agency search and compensation consultants, and so on.

Agencies will tell you they can do everything you need, and often they can. Specialists do provide useful expertise, especially for local or regional advertisers. Before you add this cost, make sure you don't have the expertise in-house or with your agency. You can also check industry associations—media, research, promotion, direct marketing, etc.

The Association of National Advertisers (ANA) provides information to its members on selecting an agency, fair compensation, and guidelines for contracts. Booklets on these subjects can be purchased by nonmembers as well. Log on to *www.ana.net*.

Another source of information, for members and nonmembers alike, is the 4As. Try *www.aaaa.org*. Local ad clubs may also have sources for you.

The stakes are high in picking a new agency. You can do it yourself, but it is time-consuming. A professional agency search team knows the territory and can help you articulate your needs and manage the process. Let's hope you don't need a new agency.

SELECTING A NEW AGENCY

If an agency has had a series of weak evaluations and has not moved vigorously to correct problems, if you've tried changing people within the agency, if there is a real reason for a change (as opposed to "a fresh look"), there is no alternative but to seek a new agency partner.

The process is time-consuming. It will involve people throughout the organization and distract from the work for current clients. It will be highly publicized. There is not that much real news in the business—the trade press and major dailies will eat it up. The whole thing will be confusing at times.

Some Things You Shouldn't Be Confused By:

Speculative Campaigns

Frequently, agencies are asked—more often, they rush forward—to create campaigns to illustrate their thinking and win the business. For starters, there is no guarantee this advertising will work in the marketplace. Often it never runs. Advertising is a collaborative process. It takes deep involvement and understanding of the business before a creative team can produce great advertising.

It's good for you to understand how an agency *thinks*. However, that can be done by asking for an agency's strategic recommendations—and simple concept boards to illustrate their points. Period.

You're not buying a campaign, you're selecting an agency. Advertisers should never select an agency based on speculative creative work alone.

Creative Awards

Recognize them for what they are—awards the industry gives to itself. Awards are seldom given for sales (Effies are a rare exception), and determining the influence of the advertising on sales is complicated. Award judges tend to favor entertainment or humor in advertising, as well as special effects or cutting-edge production techniques.

"Creative awards are immaterial and stupid," says agency head Donny Deutsch—whose agency has won a lot of awards—"because great work is work that moves your business."

Awards do have a role in attracting talent and branding an agency as "creative." Never the primary criterion for selecting an agency.

Conflicts of Interest

Conflicts are largely an emotional issue, seldom (if ever) a real one. We've never heard of any trade secrets being stolen—it's hard enough to get people to pay attention to the research and data they have in hand.

The real issue is loyalty—whose side are you on? Other professional service firms such as management consultants, lawyers, and accounting firms handle several clients in a product category. Better to look the other way on tangential conflicts than to eliminate a strong agency from consideration by being a hard-liner.

Some Things To Consider:

Define Your Needs

Put them in writing, and get agreement from all the key people who will have a say in the advertising before you look at any agencies.

- *Size*—will the agency be large enough for your needs, or so large you won't command management attention?

- *Special skills*—how important is industry knowledge, direct marketing, a global network?
- *Geography*—do you have to be in daily contact with the agency?
- *Product conflicts*—what is your policy?

If outstanding creative work is not at the head of your list, start over.

A Short Questionnaire to an Agency Short List

Pull together a list of agencies which have a point of view you respect and which appear to have an affinity for your business. People come and go. You need an organization with a business and creative philosophy, stable management, professional staff, technical expertise—a past, present, and future.

How big is the agency—and how important will you be on their client list? Does it have a credible international network, or just dots on a map? What resources are available to clients? Ask for samples of their work—in all media.

Alan Rosenshine, chairman of BBDO—*Adweek's* 2002 Agency of the Year—describes his agency's culture: "Because of our historical growth, we tend to be more entrepreneurial and turf-driven around the world. But we all share a common culture and belief in what's important—the work, the work, the work."

Select a Few Finalists

Visit the agencies—in their offices. Questionnaires won't tell you what you need to know. Meet the people who would work on your business, as well as the agency principals. Ask them to tell you about case histories in which they were personally involved. Ask them questions, so you see how they react. Spend time with them informally and individually, not just in conference rooms. Personal chemistry is important.

Do some checking. What kind of reports do you get from other clients—and former clients, from the media, from employees?

Avoid new business teams who disappear after the presentation.

Manage the Presentation

Keep the meeting small. Hold down junior level participation—this is a job for senior management. Think about how to avoid being swayed by dazzling showbiz presentations. Prohibit any finished creative work—tell agencies they will be disqualified. Concept boards with a strategy are usually enough.

Concentrate on presentations that show how an agency thinks. Give them a real company problem to address, and see how they approach it.

Give each evaluator a checklist of what you're looking for. Make a judgment about an agency's ability to contribute to the marketing strategy and, within that, to develop effective advertising. Does the agency talk about the strategy or the execution?

Leave time for Q&A—that's where you find out what people really know and how they react. And pay for their time, at least a modest fee to show good faith.

At the end of the process, you must feel comfortable with the team. They should know your business, and you should feel they have the resources to deal with tough problems. Discuss the evaluations as a group. Then wait 24 hours and make a decision. And try to live with it a long time.

What It Takes to Succeed

We've been talking about how to get great advertising, but what makes someone *personally* good at it? What does it take to succeed? Not advertising courses—the business can teach the mechanics in a few months. Not just working well with people, although it is a collaborative business, so working with others is important.

Advertising is a fast-changing business, and it takes raw intelligence to digest a steady stream of new information. You can rise to a certain level on diligence and organization, but insightful thinking is needed to lead great advertising.

The best people generate ideas and get excited about ideas. They stay in touch with popular taste. They watch TV, surf the web, and go to movies, art museums, and concerts. They read books, magazines, and newspapers (several a day). They seek patterns in market data, then try to connect the dots to create insights.

Some people are good at strategy, but less good at coming up with ideas. Others spark ideas, but are less disciplined about strategy. The best people come up with ideas and make them happen. They communicate clearly, and they know how to sell an idea.

What makes great creative people great? They are simplifiers—they peel away layers, and get to the heart. They are focused on solutions. They have a sense of "now"—what's happening in the world today, so their ideas are relevant and make a connection with the target audience that often goes beyond the advertising message. They are passionate and willing to fight for their ideas. They trust their instincts. They are risk-takers. They have a sense of fun—not many sad dogs among the great creative folks.

It is not always easy to manage top creative talent. They are often strong people with strong views. When Ted Williams was playing for the Boston Red Sox, a new manager was asked if he could get along with the volatile Williams. "Any manager who cannot get along with the last .400 hitter in baseball," he responded, "doesn't deserve to be manager."

In advertising, there are long hours filled with changes and stress. It takes stamina to bounce back after disappointments and to be able to attack the problem with fresh energy. Resilience, the ability to come back, is basic to success in all parts of the business.

A daunting list of qualities, but the people who rise to the top have most of them—plus one other. *Motivation*. They have fire in the belly.

The Client Makes the Difference

Look at the creative output of any agency—chances are the work ranges from A-plus to C-minus. The difference is usually *the client*. Since clients are the final arbiters, they are responsible for the advertising, good or bad. This responsibility underscores the need for client training, and where this book can help.

We started with David Ogilvy, so let's end with his words.

"Clients get the kind of advertising they deserve."

Glossary

Above the fold—Derived from the newspaper industry, the part of the web page that can be viewed without scrolling. This area is generally more valuable to advertisers.

ADAD (Automatic Dialing Announcement Device)—A device capable of making many telephone calls without an operator.

Adlobs—Ad-like objects, used in creative testing. More than an unadorned concept or benefit statement, less than an advertisement.

Ad network—A company that combines the inventory of many web sites into a single "network" to achieve reach and targeting capability. Revenues are split between the ad network and the web sites.

Ad server—The technology used to deliver and place ads on a publisher's web site, usually operated by a third party (such as an advertising agency) to ensure statistical validity.

Ad-Tel—A marketing service based chiefly on store scanning data.

AIDA (Attention, Interest, Desire, Action)—An early model of an effective advertising process.

AM station—A station that broadcasts through its amplitude or power rather than its frequency. An AM station can broadcast further but is received with more static and interference.

Animatics—Filmed or taped versions of storyboard drawings, for testing television commercials. ***Photomatics*** employ photographs instead of drawings.

Area of Dominant Influence (ADI)—A geographic television market as defined by Arbitron. Every county is assigned to only one ADI, based on where its highest share of viewing occurs. Similar to *DMA*.

Artwork (or **art**)—Visual material (drawing or photograph) prepared for reproduction in a print advertisement. ***Line art*** is a drawing or visual that has no tonal values, so it can be used without a halftone screen. ***Tone art*** or ***continuous tone art*** usually refers to a photograph or image.

Audio—The written description on a storyboard of what the viewer hears during the commercial, including spoken words, sound effects, and music.

Background—The part of the image that appears furthest from the viewer or on which the main image is positioned.

Banner Ad—An advertising position on a publisher's web site. Banner ads are usually linked to the advertiser's web site.

Baseline—An imaginary line on which the body of all letters rests.

Below the line—Supplementary media usually not charged to the advertising budget, such as direct marketing, public relations, or sales promotion.

Bitmap—A graphic composed of dots (also known as *pixels* or *bits*). Bitmap graphics cannot be easily scaled up or down without a loss of quality.

Bleed—That part of an image or ad that extends beyond the trim of the artwork and runs off the page, with no white border.

Blog—Short for web log. A type of web site for self-publishing (musings, etc.) and links to other web sites.

Body copy—Printed text forming the part of the ad other than headline or illustration.

Brand—The name of a product, plus characteristics that add value to a product.

Brand Development Index (BDI)—A measurement of a product's percentage of sales as a ratio (brand sales divided by population).

Brand DNA—A term used to describe the essence of a brand.

Brand equity—The value of a brand.

Brand image—The personality of a brand, including all graphic elements that make a brand's communications consistent and distinctive. Also ***brand identity***.

Brand mapping—A visualization of the positioning of a brand and its competition.

Brand name—The name of a unique product in a category.

Broadband—A high-speed connection to the internet (DSL line or cable modem).

Browser—Software used to gain access to the World Wide Web.

Bullets—A graphic device to highlight a line or paragraph, such as dots or squares.

Camera ready—Artwork that is ready for reproduction.

Campaign—A series of advertisements held together by some point of similarity.

Caption—Description of what is in a photograph or illustration, most commonly placed beneath it.

Category—A class of goods or services.

Category Development Index (CDI)—A measurement of a class of product sales as a ratio (category sales divided by population).

Cause-related marketing—A promotion that links the sale of a product or service to support a good cause.

Cinema verité—A commercial style borrowed from film documentaries, using a handheld camera and natural lighting.

Circulation—The number of copies of a magazine or newspaper that are distributed in any given issue.

Claim—Statement about the performance of a product or service. A competitive claim (e.g., more mileage) must be based on research, laboratory evidence, or other factual evidence. A subjective claim (e.g., good tasting) does not need support.

Click-through—Each time someone selects an advertiser link from a third party site in order to enter the advertiser's web site is counted as one click-through.

Click-through Rate—The number of clicks (responses) per thousand impressions. If an advertiser serves 1,000 impressions and receives 10 clicks to the site, the click-through rate is 1 percent.

Closing date—The final date to commit to the purchase of advertising space in print media.

Close-up (CU)—In film or tape, a partial view of the subject (e.g., only the head of a person). An ***extreme close-up (ECU)*** shows only the eyes.

Communications research—Research to determine whether your advertising is communicating what you want.

Composition—Percentage of a medium's total audience that is part of a specific demographic segment.

Computer imaging—Computer-generated visuals.

Concept testing—Research to determine how a product should be positioned.

Confidence level—A measure of the probability that research results would be the same if carried out again.

Control—A proven winner against which new mailings or advertisements are tested.

Conversion rate—The percent of people who move from inquiry to purchase.

Cookies—A small software program stored in the user's browser designed to identify a user or set of user preferences to a web site operator or advertiser. Commonly used to measure the number and frequency of banner ads delivered to a browser.

Copyright—Legal protection to protect a distinctive intellectual property against copies.

Cost per response—Cost of a mailing divided by the number of responses.

Cost per thousand (CPM)—Cost to reach 1,000 members of a target audience.

Coverage—Degree to which a media vehicle is able to reach an audience.

CRM (Customer Relationship Management)—A data management approach that enables organizations to identify, attract, and increase retention of profitable customers by managing relationships with them.

Crop—To use only a portion of a photograph, making the composition more interesting. Can be done on digital images in an image editing program.

Curriculum mailing—A sequence of timed mailings to a particular target.

Cut—An abrupt transition from one film scene to another.

Cutout—Addition to the surface of a billboard that may be three-dimensional.

DAGMAR (Defining Advertising Goals for Measured Results)—A testing method for advertising effectiveness.

Database—A list that goes beyond names and addresses to include demographic and psychographic information.

Daypart—Defined time periods of the broadcast day, used for analytical purposes.

Demographics—Descriptive facts about a given population group (household income, education, age, sex, etc.).

Demonstration—Visual proof that a product or service does what is claimed.

Designated Market Area (DMA)—A geographical television market as defined by Nielsen. Similar to ***ADI.***

Die cut—To cut paper or cardboard with a metal die to create a particular design or shape in a printed page as an intentional part of the design.

Digital television—A TV signal based on digital (rather than analog) technology, producing better quality reception.

Display allowance—Money given to the retailer by the manufacturer in return for space to put up a display.

Dissolve—A gradual transition from one film scene to another, often to denote passage of time.

Domain name—The unique designation for a web site. Typically, domain names "mirror" their offline brands. Examples: *CNN.com* or *Tide.com*.

Downtest—Creating a less expensive mailing package by dropping one or more elements, and testing it against the control.

Duplication—Percentage of people who see a message in more than one medium. In direct marketing, it is the appearance of the same name on more than one mailing list.

DV (Direct Voice)—Indication on a storyboard that someone is speaking "on camera."

E-commerce—A business model based on internet (rather than retail) transactions.

Emotional benefit—A nonrational consumer benefit that suggests how a consumer feels about using a product or service.

EPS (Encapsulated PostScript)—A graphic format containing both vector and bitmap graphics that can be scaled up or down without loss of quality.

FCC (Federal Communications Commission)—Agency that regulates broadcasting.

FDA (Food and Drug Administration)—Agency that regulates advertising of foods, drugs, and cosmetics.

Fiber optic cable—Thin glass fibers bundled together in cables to transmit digital information by means of light pulses.

Flanker—A brand that supports a core brand by acting as a barrier against competition.

Flash—A software program developed by Macromedia Corporation for the creation of sophisticated animation and multimedia. Used by many advertisers to enhance the production and presentation value of banner advertising.

Flighting—The concentration of advertising into bursts of several weeks, with no advertising (***hiatus***) in between.

FM station—A radio station that broadcasts by modifying its frequency, resulting in high fidelity reception.

Focus group session—A group of people selected from a target audience, led by a skilled moderator, expresses attitudes about product, services, or other topics.

Folio—Refers to the page number.

Font—A complete set of characters in one typeface. A typeface can be comprised of many fonts.

Four-color process—The printing method that combines four colors (cyan, magenta, yellow, black) to create a gamut of thousands of colors.

Frequency—Number of times a message is potentially seen or heard in a defined period of time.

Frequency distribution—The number of times individuals are exposed to advertising in a schedule.

Fringe time—Off-peak TV hours that are less expensive than prime time.

FSI (free-standing insert)—A separate printed page or pages with advertisements and coupons, usually distributed within a newspaper.

FTC (Federal Trade Commission)—Agency that enforces truth in advertising.

Fulfillment—Redemption of an offer, such as turning in coupons.

Gatefold—The expansion to a magazine page that can be opened or unfolded.

Geo-demographic systems—Sophisticated databases that store information on population groups.

Gross impressions—Total number of messages delivered by a media plan.

Gross rating points (GRPs)—Total of all rating points achieved for a specific schedule or campaign.

Halftone—Process by which a continuous tone photograph or illustration is converted to a dot pattern for printing. Generally created digitally via scanning.

Hits—On the internet, number of page views recorded.

Hiatus—A period of no advertising.

High ground—In most categories, the one benefit more important than any other.

Home page takeover—An internet advertising message that dominates the publisher's home page for a short time before resolving to a subordinate position.

Hot spot—A place in a catalog or letter that attracts extra readership. Also, the upper left corner of an e-mail—seen in the e-mail preview window.

HTML (Hypertext Markup Language)—The software code used to build web sites.

HTTP (Hypertext Transfer Protocol)—The standard methodology by which web browsers communicate with web servers.

HUT—The percent of Homes Using Television at any given time.

Image—The subject (photograph, illustration, title treatment, etc.) to be reproduced in print.

Inbound—The use of 800 (free) or 900 (toll) phone numbers allowing consumers to place an order from a mailing or advertisement.

Index—Shows the relationship of two concepts numerically.

Infomercial—A program-length TV direct response commercial (generally 30 minutes), run in non-prime hours.

Insert (or **tip-in**)—A preprinted advertisement of one or more pages bound into a publication.

Interactive television—Technology that permits viewers to interact directly with TV and request products and services.

Internet—The worldwide collection of networks and computer devices connected to one another through a common protocol called TCP/IP (Transmission control protocol/internet protocol).

Interstitial—Any advertising or promotional message inserted between TV programs. On the internet, advertising displayed between one page and another.

Intranet—An internal computer network that gives employees access to the same databases.

Johnson Box—At the top of a direct mail letter (occasionally in a box), a sentence or two about the incentive and the reply date.

Justified type—Lines set as "justified" all have the same line length, so they line up evenly on left and right.

Kern—The adjustment of space between two printed characters to push them together or force them apart.

Keyline—A rectangle drawn in the space where a photograph should go. The line itself does not print, it just shows the position and size of the photo.

Key visual—One frame that captures the main thrust of a commercial.

Landscape—Printing on a page that is wider than it is tall.

Layout—A general appearance of what the finished print advertisement will look like, indicating the relationship between the text and graphic images.

Leader boards—Large format internet banners dominating the top of a web page.

Line extension—Products that bear the same parent brand name and offer the consumer varied options (e.g., Diet Coke). Also known as "flankers."

Logotype (or **logo**)—The visual identity or stylistic treatment of a brand name.

Long shot—In film or tape, a scene that takes in the full view of the subject (e.g., the entire body of a person). A ***medium shot***, from the waist up.

Mailing list—Names of people with some kinship, such as subscribers to a magazine.

Make good—An advertisement run as a replacement for one that was scheduled but did not run, or ran incorrectly.

Market share—The percentage held by one brand of all sales in a category.

Mechanical—The final assembly of all the composed elements in a printed piece. (Also, ***camera-ready***; produced digitally, known as a ***digital mechanical***.)

Media—Forms of communication providing news and entertainment, usually together with advertising.

Merge-purge—When two or more mailing lists are combined or merged, duplicate names are weeded out.

Microsite—A special internet advertising section linked from a publisher's web site.

Mock-up—A rough sample of an ad, publication, or package design to visualize the size, color, and mechanics of the final piece.

Model release—Legal form signed by the photographer's subject to permit reproduction of the likeness.

Niche brand—A brand directed to a smaller target audience, providing specific benefits to that group.

On-air recall—A measure of commercial effectiveness based on asking viewers what they remember about a commercial aired 24 hours previously.

Offline—Advertising *not* on the internet.

Opt-in—The act of consciously choosing to receive particular e-mails. Opt-in lists are typically more valuable than Opt-out lists because users have taken an action to receive the material.

Opt-out—The act of choosing not to receive particular e-mails. Opt-out requires that users take an action to remove their name from an e-mail list.

Outbound—Use of a telephone to sell a product or service or to close a sale previously made in a mailing or advertisement.

Out of register—A blurred printed image resulting from a plate reproducing slightly above or to the side of the matching plate underneath it.

Page-view—A web page displayed to a single user. If *NYTimes.com* generates 300 million page-views per month, this means 300 million individual pages were displayed to all users of the site. Multiply the number of monthly page views by the number of ads per page to measure total banner ad inventory for a site in a given month.

Pay per click—A form of compensation whereby the advertiser pays a set amount for each click-through.

Penetration—The proportion of persons (or homes) that are physically able to be exposed to a medium.

Perceptual mapping—A grouping of a number of brands that offer similar benefits.

Personality—Another term for the tone and manner of an advertisement.

Persuasion testing—A measure of commercial effectiveness based on measuring how a commercial will affect a consumer's likelihood to buy a product or service.

Plate—A flat sheet of metal bearing a design or image from which an impression or reproduction is printed.

POP (point of purchase)—Display or other materials in store.

Pop-under—A form of web advertising that creates a second browser window that is loaded "under" the web page selected by the user. When users exit from their primary browser, the pop-under remains on the screen.

Pop-up—A form of web advertising that appears in a second browser window over the primary web display. Considered among the most intrusive forms of web advertising. In magazines, paper or other material cut to represent a visual, then folded flat and glued into the publication. When the reader reaches this page, the visual "pops up."

Portrait—A page that is taller than it is wide.

POS (Point of Sale)—Another designation for Point of Purchase.

Positioning—The place held by a product or service in the consumer's mind.

Post analysis—Comparison of the actual gross impressions delivered versus the original estimates, after the schedule has run.

Presenter—A spokesperson on camera.

Primary audience—Number of readers who get a publication at a newsstand or receive it as a subscriber at home. ***Secondary*** or ***passalong audience*** is the number of readers exposed to the publication other than by direct purchase.

Primary research—Research that involves collecting original data on a specific issue.

Printing—There are five basic methods. ***Letterpress***, in which the printing surface is raised and pressed against the paper. ***Gravure***, in which the printing surface is depressed. ***Lithography*** (or ***offset***), in which the image is first printed on a rubber roller or blanket, then offset onto paper. ***Screen*** or ***silk screen***, which uses a printing stencil. ***Digital***, in which toner or pigment is heat-set onto the printing surface.

Privacy policy—The stated set of rules that a web site owner applies to the collection and application of personal consumer information.

Process color—Color made up of the CMYK colors (cyan, magenta, yellow, black).

Promise—A summary statement of the benefits of the product.

Promise testing—Research to determine the most important and meaningful benefit offered in a product.

Proof—A reproduced version of an image or advertisement. The first one is a ***loose proof*** or ***color correction proof***, pulled for checking the color reproduction of images and illustrations. The second is a ***repro*** or ***content proof***, pulled so all the content can be checked and proofread. This would include all type, logos, images, etc. The content proof is usually accompanied by a final color proof as well.

PSA (public service announcement)—A commercial for a social or community cause, broadcast by TV stations at no cost.

Psychographics—Information such as values or lifestyles about a given group in the population.

Publisher (web)—A content provider on the internet.

Pulsing—Continuous advertising, with periodic bursts.

PUT—Percentage of People Using Television at any given time.

PVR (personal video recorder)—A device that can be set to record TV programs on a schedule.

Qualitative research—Research to probe the reasons why people act or how they think. Generally smaller sample sizes and not projectable.

Quantitative research—Research to quantify (with larger sample sizes) qualitative research or other marketing hypotheses.

Quintile analysis—The average frequency in each of five equal groups, used to evaluate the degree of impact of a media effort.

Rating—Percentage of homes or individuals tuned in to the average quarter-hour of a program.

Rational benefit—A statement of a brand's logical objective benefits.

Reach—Number of different persons who see or hear a message at least once. Also known as ***cume***, ***unduplicated***, or ***net*** audience.

Registered mark—A legal definition of a distinctive visual sign that represents a business (usually the brand name) and protects it against copies.

Registration—In printing, the correct positioning of one color on another. On the internet, the act of providing some personal information (zip code, e-mail address) in return for a unique user ID and password allowing access to a web site. Registration data is typically used for advertising targeting.

Resolution—The quality of graphics expressed in the number of "dots" (or bits or pixels). A high-resolution graphic has more dots per inch (*dpi*) while a low-resolution graphic has a lower dpi. Resolution applies both to graphics designed for print (typically high resolution) and for the web (low resolution).

Retail branding—Brand identity for a retailer's own-label goods.

Rich media—Web site advertising that incorporates advanced multimedia characteristics and interactivity.

Rotoscoping—Film technique that combines animation with live action.

Rough cut—Early stage in the editing of a commercial.

Run-of-press (ROP)—A print position request to run an advertisement anywhere in the publication.

Run-of-schedule (ROS)—A broadcast position request to run a commercial any time of day or night.

Sales promotion—A marketing technique to increase sales, usually though couponing, sweepstakes, contests, gifts or premiums, rebates, in-store displays.

SEC (Securities and Exchange Commission)—Agency that regulates advertising for stocks and bonds.

Secondary research—Research that uses published information and data.

Serif—In typography, a thin line that projects above and below certain letters.

Session—Sometimes called a "visit." The number of pages used during an individual web site experience, usually beginning with the home page.

SFX (sound effects)—Sounds that are added after a commercial has been filmed.

Share—In broadcast, the audience of a program as a percentage of all households using the medium at the time.

Share-of-Voice (SOV)—The number of times the audience sees or hears a brand's message, in relation to all competitive messages.

Sheet—In outdoor, a reference to the days when printing couldn't handle large sheets of paper. A *30-sheet board* now means a size (about 10 feet by 22 feet), no longer 30 sheets of paper.

Shockwave—A software program used to create rich media web sites.

Shooting board—A detailed version of a storyboard showing shot by shot what will be filmed or taped.

Shot—In film or tape, usually one scene.

Showing—In outdoor and transit, the number of posters that can be seen by the adult population of one area in one day.

Simmons/MRI—Syndicated information about the buying and media habits of different population groups.

Skyscraper—A vertical banner ad format, typically extending along the columns of a web page.

Site session—A type of online advertising buy in which the advertiser buys the entire advertising inventory of a given site for a prescribed time period.

Slice-of-life—A commercial that uses a realistic situation and natural language to simulate real life.

Slotting allowance—Money paid by the manufacturer to the retailer (usually for a new product), to gain access to the computerized system and shelf space.

Snipe—Overlay to an existing billboard, usually to add information.

Soho—Small office/home office.

Sound design—All elements of the sound track, including music, sound effects, and background noises.

Sound track—The audio portion of a commercial. A combination of ***voice track***, ***music track***, and ***effects track***.

Spam—Usually refers to unwanted e-mail, often from direct-response advertisers.

Spectaculars—Elaborate billboards that go beyond the usual two-dimensional rectangle.

Split-run—Different versions of an advertisement in the same issue of a publication, for testing.

Spot advertising—Broadcast media purchased on a market-by-market basis.

Spot color—Solid colors not using the CMYK process colors. The ***Pantone Matching System (PMS)*** is the best-known system of spot colors used in graphic design.

Spread (or **double-truck**)—Two facing pages in a publication.

Standard Advertising Unit (SAU)—A system of unit sizes in newspaper advertising.

Stock music—Existing music that can be purchased for an agreed-upon usage.

Stock photo—Photograph taken previously that can be purchased for agreed-upon usage.

Storyboard—Drawings that depict the action of a commercial, together with a written description of what the viewer will see and hear.

Strategy—A written plan that charts the course of action for marketing a brand.

Streaming media—Typically refers to video or sound delivered through a media player on the internet.

Sub-brand—A product that is part of a line of goods and uses the core brand as a parent name (e.g., Diet Pepsi).

Support—A reason for the consumer to believe your claim.

Surround session—A type of online advertising buy in which the advertiser buys exclusive access (all of the advertising positions) to a user's session on a particular web site.

T-scope (tachistoscope)—An instrument that evaluates the effectiveness of an advertisement, poster, or package by measuring eye movements.

Take-ones—Brochures in a counter display or pads of tear-off blanks pasted on transit posters.

Target audience—Primary prospects sought by an advertiser.

Telemarketing—Use of the telephone to sell or buy.

Test marketing—Tracking the sales of a new or improved product in one or more cities before marketing it more broadly.

Testimonial—A commercial using real people to endorse a product.

TIFF (Tagged Image Files Format)—A bitmap graphic file format, one of the most widely used bitmap graphic formats. Since TIFF is a bitmap format, it cannot scale up or down without loss of quality.

Tone and manner—In a creative strategy, the statement of how the advertising should project the brand's image or personality.

Tracking study—Continuous in-market research that monitors a brand's performance (including sales and attitudes) against competition.

Trial-builder—A promotion aimed at generating purchase by new users.

True value concept—In direct marketing, the measurable long-term value of a customer.

Typeface—A style of lettering used in print, on TV, or on the web. This book is set in Sabon, for example. One typeface includes all the various fonts in that style.

Typo—An unintentional mistake in spelling.

Unique visitors—The number of individual users who come to a web site during a given time period.

UPC (Universal Product Code)—A code printed on products that reveals information when scanned electronically.

Upper case—Capital letters, as opposed to ***lower case***, or noncapitalized letters.

URL (Uniform Resource Locator)—A web address, comparable in the physical world to a house address. All web sites have URLs just as every house has a unique street address.

VALS (Values and Lifestyles)—A syndicated system for sorting consumers into different lifestyle groups, and linking their behavior to their values.

 VCR—Videocassette recorder.

Vector—Unlike bitmap graphics, vector graphics are composed of lines and curves. This means vector graphics can be scaled up or down without loss in quality.

Velox—A high-resolution paper positive of a digital file. Even though veloxes are high resolution, they can only hold around 85 LPI (lines per inch) and are generally used for newspaper ads or designs that have no register.

Verbatims—The exact words used by people when asked to comment on rough or finished commercials.

Video—The written description on a storyboard of the visual flow of a commercial.

Viewers per household—The average number of persons watching or listening to a program in each home.

Viral marketing—An internet term for "word-of-mouth" advertising, consumer-to-consumer dialogue that distributes and amplifies a message.

VO (Voice-over)—Indication on a storyboard that someone is speaking "off camera."

Weasels—Wording in an advertisement that deliberately suggests the product does something it may not do.

Web Log (Blog)—Self-publishing on the web, usually characterized by regular updates, including personal thoughts and web links.

World Wide Web (www)—A global network of servers on the internet that allows any user with a browser to access specially formatted documents called web pages.

Wire frame—An outline for a web site, showing the navigation and initial content for each page of a web site with no design or animation. A way to test concept, copy, and usability at an early stage.

Zap—Obliterating a taped commercial by fast-forwarding with a remote control device.

Index

About the Authors

Collaborative Animals

Kenneth Roman, former Chairman and Chief Executive of Ogilvy & Mather Worldwide, one of the top international advertising and communications firms, is also the co-author of *Writing That Works.*

Jane Maas, a Creative Director at Ogilvy & Mather and subsequently Chairman of the Earle Palmer Brown agency, is a strategic and creative consultant and conducts sessions for the Association of National Advertisers on how to get more effective advertising. She is the author of *Adventures of an Advertising Woman.*

The authors are collaborative animals who worked together successfully on major advertising campaigns . . . and this book. They have been joined in this Third Edition by Martin Nisenholtz, CEO of New York Times Digital. At Ogilvy & Mather, he founded the first group devoted specifically to interactive communications. Prior to his current assignment, he was President of The New York Times Electronic Media Company and director of content strategy for Ameritech Corporation. He is a director of the Interactive Advertising Bureau and chairman of the Online Publishers Association.

Acknowledgments

Thank You!

Heather Higgins, for major contributions to the Integrated Communications and Direct Marketing chapters, and elsewhere throughout the book.

Toni Maloney, Graham Phillips, Ellen Roman, and Marc Schiller, for reviewing the entire manuscript (and improving it).

Jess Aguirre, Dana Allen, Marsha Appel, Nadine Bauman, Bill Begina, Mary Bennett, Cathy Black, Mike Bower, Ken Caffrey, Craig Calder, Diane Cimini, Larry Cole, Patrick Collins, Shari Dalconzo, Carol David, Gene DeWitt, Gary Freas, Anita Galvin, Denise Garcia, Connie Garrido, Mindy Goldberg, David Gooder, Barbara Greenberg, Karen Harvey, John Hayes, Steve Horne, Cathleen Hunter, Rick Isaacson, Jim Jenkins, Linda Kelly, Jason Krebs, Paul Kurnit, MaryEllen LaManna, Steve Lance, Ken Lantz, Doug Leeds, Terry Lisbon, Michael Logan, Jerry McGee, Geoff Meredith, Annette Minkalis, Bernie Novgorodoff, Ken Olshan, John Overfield, Pierce Pelouze, Jerry Pickholz, Paula Pierce, Sharon Poff, Gordon Rademaker, Elaine Reiss, Judy Ricker, Tom Sassos, Jerry Thomas, Jim Warner, Tom Wright, and Michael Zimbalist—for your contributions and insights.

You are very much our co-authors.

'NICE ALTOIDS'

IBM
@too
IBM is an IBM e-business

Speed bump.
The new Turbo
Drivers wanted.

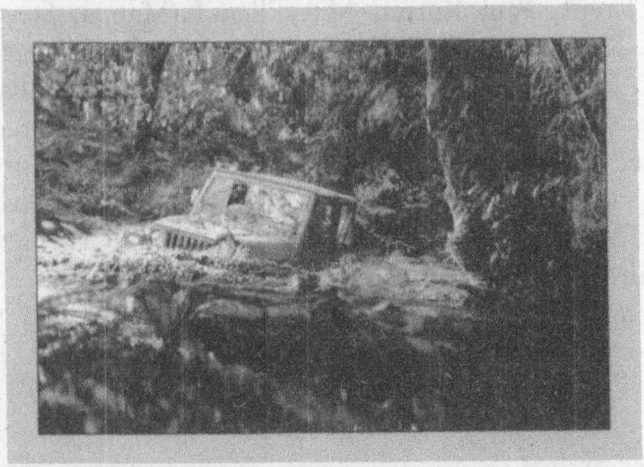